SUSTAINABILITY AND SPIRITUALITY

SUSTAINABILITY
AND
SPIRITUALITY

John E. Carroll

State University of New York Press

Published by
State University of New York Press, Albany

For information, address State University of New York Press,
90 State Street, Suite 700, Albany, NY 12207

Production by Judith Block
Marketing by Michael Campochiaro

Library of Congress Cataloging-in-Publication Data

Carroll, John E. (John Edward), 1944–
    Sustainability and spirituality / by John E. Carroll
        p. cm.
    Includes bibliographical references and index.
    ISBN 0-7914-6177-7 (alk. paper) — ISBN 0-7914-6178-5 (pbk. : alk. paper)
        1. Human ecology—Religious aspects.   2. Nature conservation—Religious aspects.
    I. Title.

BL65.E36C37 2004
201'.77—dc22
                                                            2003190067

10 9 8 7 6 5 4 3 2 1

This book is dedicated to the American women, religious and lay, who are compellingly showing us the way to an ecologically sustainable future. Quietly, gently, humbly, but with conviction, determination and passion, they are demonstrating how to live with ecological principles and how to carry out the Great Work.

*There comes a time when each of us needs
to celebrate miracles when we see them.*

—Seamus Heaney

CONTENTS

FOREWORD

Some people might find it odd that John Carroll turns to a diverse collection of monasteries and convents for his examples of environmentally sustainable communities in this country. But on only a moment's reflection, it makes real sense.

For one thing, religious communities have always been interested in long-term survival—looking backward, that almost seems their raison d'être. Who, after all, tended the flickering flame of civilization for the centuries of the Dark Ages? In our time, too, survival is called into question. One need not be paranoid to sense that our arrangements are fragile, vulnerable (certainly not after 9/11, when our biggest and sturdiest buildings simply vanished). A dozen ranking ecologists have issued warnings in recent years that we are overshooting our limits, accelerating toward a cliff—pick your metaphor. And so the urge toward a kind of self-sufficiency, toward closed loops of food and energy. In people driven by personal fear, this takes tragic form: bomb shelters, weapons caches. In people driven by faith and love and hope, it takes the forms outlined here.

But of course a sense of approaching peril is not the main motivation for these communities. Instead, it is an affection for God's world, and God's creations, man included. For anyone holding such affection, these can be difficult times: if you really think about what extinction represents, or if you have witnessed what it means to be truly poor in the shadow of a rich world, then you have, no doubt, wanted to do something useful about it. And, no doubt, tried—joined organizations, written letters.

But most of us are almost hopelessly tangled in the various systems of our world—the need to make a living, the need to keep up appearances, the need in a stressed life to take pleasure from things. And it is here, perhaps, that religious communities really can show us the way. Not only are the convents and monasteries that Carroll profiles busy figuring out how to meet their own needs themselves, they are also busy making sure those needs aren't too large to meet. In the monastic tradition of joyful simplicity and pooled resources, they have found some of the secrets to real sustainability. Not, as Carroll points out, the ersatz "sustainable growth" of the politicians, eager to paint a green tinge on business as usual. Or even the wistful eco-consciousness of the guy with a Sierra Club sticker pasted on the back of his SUV. But the actual two-sides-to-the-equation effort at sustainability that getting ourselves out of our current pickle will require. One way to say it is: solar panels still aren't quite efficient or cheap enough to generate all the electricity a home could require. The ones on our roof, for instance, supply about half our juice. But if we could cut our needs in half . . . And we probably could, especially if we were living in some of the ways outlined in this engaging piece of reporting.

None of this would mean anything if life in these communities were long-faced, grim, and mournful. But by Carroll's account, and my own more limited experiences, it is anything but. Rich in the good things of the modern world—conversation, humor. But rich also in the things that so many of us pine for: actual silence, physical work, rest, companionship.

Carroll begins his journey looking for examples of environmental sustainability, and I think he has found them—more convincing examples than people who have looked in more obvious and secular places. But along the way he has also found something related, and just as important: examples of human sustainability, hints about ways that we might reshape our attitudes as compelling as our kitchens and gardens and boilers.

Bill McKibben
Ripton, Vermont

ACKNOWLEDGMENTS

For research assistance in the field, I am indebted to Sr. Phyllis Plantenberg, O.S.B., Mark Dodson, Antonio Lujan, Darryl Birkenfeld, Lydia Villanueva, and Rob Gorman. For manuscript review assistance, I am indebted to Sr. Miriam Therese MacGillis, O.P., Sr. Gail Worcelo, C.P., Fr. Thomas Berry, C.P., and Beth Fisher. For devoted clerical assistance, I thank Linda Scogin, and for all-around assistance over the nine years of this project, I am indebted to my wife, Diana Carroll.

I am also grateful to the University of New Hampshire for awarding me an important sabbatical leave to conclude the research on this project, and to the Farrington Fund of the Department of Natural Resources of the University of New Hampshire for financial assistance.

Chapter One

INTRODUCTION

"Sustainability" is an all too common word describing a condition which these days seems to hardly exist. Indeed, the extremely common usage of the word may be symptomatic of a deeper realization that the condition of sustainability, which most people would posit as both necessary and good, is nearly nonexistent. In fact, most usage of the word "sustainability," it could be argued, whether by institutions or by individuals, refers to a shallow superficial and cosmetic form of sustainability which does not reflect sustainability at all and is inaccurate, perhaps even dishonest, in its usage. Can true sustainability, for example, be based on a foundation of nonrenewable natural resources such as fossil fuels? Not likely, and yet fossil fuels underly virtually everything we do, the entirety of the way we live, and the value system we live by. Can true sustainability be based on an energy intensive profligate wasteful lifestyle such as the world has never seen before? Not likely. Can true sustainability be based on a value system which, at best, concerns itself with miles per gallon in a motor vehicle but never questions how or for what purpose a vehicle is being used, who or what it is transporting and why? Not with any application of honesty. Can true sustainability be related to a consumptive lifestyle that seems to know no limit (and refuses to consider any concept of limits), a lifestyle predicated on growth for its own sake (the disease of "growthism," which is what unrestrained capitalism is all about)? No, not if we are rational.

Steven C. Rockefeller has written that an activity is sustainable if it can be continued indefinitely. According to Rockefeller, "Patterns of production and consumption are considered to be ecologically sustainable if

1

they respect and safeguard the regenerative capacities of our oceans, rivers, forests, farmlands, and grasslands. . . . (S)ustainability includes all the interrelated activities that promote the long-term flourishing of Earth's human and ecological communities."[1]

Sustainability, therefore, according to the true sense of the word, requires far more from us than the cheap, shallow, and superficial measures commonly taken under the guise of sustainability, measures such as those in agriculture and food systems, in energy and in other ways we utilize and/or relate to the Creation. True sustainability requires a change in our fundamental values, it requires us to be fundamentally countercultural and revolutionary, at least as to the common culture and its evolution since the Second World War, if not earlier.

A monk of my acquaintance in Minnesota once remarked to me that sustainability is a conversion experience. The secular world might scoff at this, figuring that a phrase like "conversion experience" might be what one would expect from a monk, priest, or clergyman. And yet, when one thinks about it, such a "conversion experience" is precisely what is called for if we are to meet the expectations of our own rationality. Surely, a true change in our system of values, if that is indeed what is called for, could only occur as a conversion experience, for it would necessitate a fundamental change from deep within us. Not simply to alter how we do things but to change the value presupposition of why we do things is a conversion of the deepest kind.

If, therefore, we argue that sustainability of necessity is a conversion experience, if it is and must be predicated on a deep change of values themselves, and not on a halfhearted patch-it-up enterprise, then its expectation cannot be lodged in the prevailing value system, the "dominant paradigm" as it is called. It must come from a deeper place.

With these things in mind we might ask where we might find models of real sustainability. The location of such models should correlate to people who put their faith in values other than those found within the dominant value system. They should be found among people who have developed a deep spirituality, a transcendent spirituality. They should be found among people who place their faith in something bigger than they are, in contrast to those who commonly place their faith in things smaller than they are (the latter including, for example, the mall, shopping, consumption, the car, science, technology, the "techno-fix," economic growth, "growthism," money, power, and so forth, any or all of which might readily become gods or idols in people's lives). In contrast, those who place their faith in things bigger than they are, things that transcend them, things that were there before them, things that will be there after them, things beyond their ability to encapsulate or comprehend, to know or to de-limit, whether one God, multiple gods, mystery, nature, the cosmos, and so forth, might demonstrate a greater ability to recognize, to demonstrate, to practice, to truly know sustainability.

Where might we have hope of finding such countercultural behavior, such sustainable behavior? One such place might be among people of faith. We might find such behavior not necessarily among "people of faith" in the narrow reduced way the world too often defines such people, that is, members of churches, baptized persons, persons who make claims about faith, though the phrase can include them. But we might find it in people deeply spiritual (whether that spirituality shows itself or not) who do have faith in mystery, in something which is not them, and which transcends their being. A possible place for the evolution and maturation of true values of sustainability, therefore, might be in communities of such people, in "faith communities," but would not likely be inclusive of all people in such communities, for such communities are part of the same distorted unsustainable culture in which all of us, to a greater or lesser degree, live our lives.

Some such people might call themselves Christian. (If one follows Jesus Christ to the Crucifixion, one might argue a lack of sustainability, but then there is the Resurrection, a very different story.) No doubt Jesus Christ was a practitioner par excellence of countercultural behavior, of radicalism, of revolution. And capital punishment was a natural response by the society of his day. That society knew an enemy, a troublemaker of serious proportions, when it saw one, and acted accordingly (albeit while running the risk of creating a martyr, which it did and which has been done since). So, sustainability might be found within or among some groups of Christians, for Christians claim to believe in a transcendent God, and also believe in immanence, of the Creator in the created, of God in all, and, therefore, ideally, of the sacrality of all things. They believe in the Great Chain of Being, to quote Thomas Aquinas.

The oft-quoted biblical directive that God has given humankind dominion over the Earth is taken by all herein to mean humankind collectively, not individually, and for all time over all coming as well as past generations. This allows human beings no claim that the Creation is simply here for our use to do with as we will.

Monastics of all stripes, Christian, Hindu, Buddhist, are by definition (and at their ideal) also countercultural. For the Christian-related reasons already alluded to, and for other reasons, one might hope to find some true sustainability among them. However, in addition to being human, they are not totally removed from our culture or the times in which we all live, so they might not always yield good models. But the potential is there.

Indigenous or aboriginal peoples, with their earth-centered reverence for the Creation, for the sacrality of all, with creation-oriented traditions evolving over many centuries, might also be a place to seek models of sustainability, models which are spiritually based. In addition to being part of the antisustainable, antiecological corruptions of our own times and our world, however, indigenous peoples often have an additional heavy burden, the yolk of many generations of oppression and destruction of their culture which leaves so many of them incapable of carrying leadership responsibility. They are just too weighted down. But countercultural as they are, we should not ignore them as models. Likewise, one can look to the wisdom of classical civilizations, to the wisdom of science, to the wisdom of women, as Thomas Berry, in his books *Dream of the Earth* and *The Great Work*, has done.

There are undoubtedly other places to look for true models of sustainability.

This volume suggests that:

- The way to achieve environmental sustainability is through ecological living. The way to achieve ecological living is ultimately through spirituality.

- The changeover to ecological living requires a conversion away from the dominant paradigm or value system of our culture, and the active development of resistance to that value system.

- Such changeover requires rejection of that value system, the rejection of consumption and waste as a lifestyle, and the embrace of frugality as a core principle.

As to spirituality, the word refers to the condition of being of the spirit. The spirit is that part of us which animates us, which gives us life. It is that part of us which seeks transcendence, mystery, the other, that which seeks the BIG picture. It provides an essential faith in the future, a grounding for hope. It gives us the determination to persist and prevail. It has been said that when we lose our cosmology, our relation to the whole, to that BIG picture, we get small and settle for shopping malls.

This volume seeks first to gain a handle on a clear and undistorted meaning of the term "sustainability," as informed by faith belief. Chapter two presents parameters of the possible meaning of the term "sustainability." In Chapter three, five outstanding examples of spiritually-driven and faith-based community models of sustainability in five states are presented to the reader. The important philosophical foundation of the thought of Thomas Berry, fundamental to many of the models of sustainability presented in this book, is then described and discussed in chapter four. Chapter five presents the application and actualization of this thought, as carried out in the work of the Sisters of Earth network. The role of the long-established and countercultural system of monasticism, in its Christian or Western form, and the relationship of that system and its Rule to the land and to ecology, are discussed in chapter six. An understanding of the interpretation of science as practiced by spiritually grounded and creation-centered religious and their lay colleagues, is important. Chapter seven is devoted to this subject. The seminal role of social justice and its modern day evolution into eco-justice as basic to both the practice of ecological thought and to Christianity justifies the attention given in chapter eight. A word on where this work is evolving and a description of the establishment, as an outcome of the ideas developed in this book, of the world's first "Ecozoic Monastery" (chapter nine) concludes the volume.

The many models described in this volume not only represent the tangible link between ecology and spirituality, a survey of what is, but, more importantly, they represent a vision of what could be. We can use all the vision we can get, and a broad integrated focus on such models of eco-spirituality is what this work is all about.[2]

Chapter Two

ON SUSTAINABILITY, RELIGION, AND ECOLOGY

Spiritually based sustainable living is an endless dance of reason and faith. Reason without faith succumbs to pride, arrogance, hubris, and all that that brings with it, while faith without reason denies humanity, denies who we are as human beings. Sustainability without attention to Mystery, Spirit, and Spirituality is a dead end street, for it ignores who we are.

During the decade of the 1990s a significant new dialogue developed at the interface of ecology and religion. The concept of such an interface is now emerging within the formal study of ecology, environmental science, environmental affairs (policy, law, economics), and natural resource management. It is to fill the need of text in this area for the benefit of both students and practitioners of environmental conservation, natural resource management, and development that this volume has been written.

The purpose of this chapter is to portray the philosophical undercurrents which bely the treatment of sustainability, religion, and ecology, which this book is about. Insight into these undercurrents is fundamental to an understanding of the spiritually grounded, faith-based communities of sustainability described in the chapters following. Indigenous peoples' spiritualities and Eastern philosophies, especially as they relate to Judaeo-Christianity, are important considerations, but it is Judaeo-Christianity itself which has been dominantly formative in the American character. Thus, it is this religious form and direction which will be most

6

useful to the understanding of the reader and it is the area, therefore, which deserves emphasis.

FAITH AND REASON

In Western society and culture, which effectively means today global society and culture, science and religion are re-converging after some four centuries of separation. Before Galileo the two had been one. Since Galileo, and particularly with the re-enforcing dualistic philosophies of Descartes, Newton, Bacon, and others, the two have been separate and apart. At the dawn of the twenty-first century, evidence is clear that this separation no longer works in the interest of humankind or human society. It is also clear that the separation is no longer sustainable in the belief or value system of larger and larger numbers of people. Some in our society are fearful of this reconvergence and what it means; others are welcoming and believe its time has come. Regardless of how one feels about what should be, it is clear that the four century old dualism has run its course; it no longer provides a valid story or myth to guide us. It is being replaced by a wholism more in keeping with the findings of science, especially ecology and quantum physics/quantum mechanics, and with the current stage of our human development.

It is also clear that student and general public interest in the subject of ecological or environmental ethics and values in general, and in religion, in religious values and in spirituality and spiritual values in particular, is increasing in this new century. This increased interest is a reversal from steadily waning interest in these areas for many of the earlier and middle decades of the twentieth century. And, while some of this increased or renewed interest in religion is narrow, specific, and dogmatic, that is, fundamentalist in nature, an enormous amount of it focuses on much broader aspects of the subject, more commonly focusing on spirituality, or more broadly defined spiritual values. This includes a search for meaning, for spiritual meaning, in what had become, in the perception of many, a spiritually impoverished and meaningless existence in a similarly de-mystified and meaningless world. There is clearly in this experience a reconvergence of mystery with the human spirit.

Sharply increased interest in and discourse on matters lying at the interface of ecological principles and spiritual values is spreading to many different activists and decision makers. They range from Catholic and

Protestant theologians teaching in colleges, universities, seminaries, and divinity schools; to religious studies professionals engaged in teaching and praxis; and to assorted clerics, pastors, pastoral ministers, rabbis in parishes, congregations, various church or church-related institutions. Books, including my own *Embracing Earth: Catholic Approaches to Ecology, The Greening of Faith: God, the Environment and the Good Life,* and *Ecology and Religion: Scientists Speak,* are among many teaching aids and guides now being produced to serve this demand. Video and audiocassettes are also being sold in record numbers in this field. Likewise, there are increasing numbers of scientists moving into work at this interface, albeit at a somewhat slower pace than their theological kin.

The source of ecology is the Greek word *"oikos,"* meaning home in the broadest sense; the source of religion is the Latin word *"religio,"* a binding together, including with roots or origins, to creator in the broadest sense. The two together generate ecological ethics and values, the base for sustainability.

When the idea of ecology (*oikos*) and the idea of religion (*religio*) are congruent with one another, when they flow together as in the confluence of two rivers, synthesis results. The question we must ask is how would we know this congruence, this synthesis, how would it demonstrate itself, what would it look like? If spirituality and sustainability is a story of the confluence of two powerful ideas, rivers of thought, that of ecological science, ecology and ecological thought, with that of moral choice, of religion, of religious doctrine, of spirituality, how might one expect to witness it in practical working models in the real world? What would such models look like? Among others, communities of women religious, monastic communities, and both church-related and secular social justice projects are being considered to find an answer. Might some such communities epitomize the confluence and congruence of these two rivers of thought at the dawn of the twenty-first century? What then happens in practice when the two flow together?

The centerpiece of ecology is *oikos,* the Greek word for home. The word "ecology" literally means earth logic, earth wisdom, the wisdom of the home. Home in the true sense means the entirety, the totality, of the environment in which we exist, in effect the cosmos, of which we know very little and about which we are learning. And a central feature of what we have learned through modern science is that, within the order that humans can know and measure, that is, within the phenomenal order, the universe is the only text without a context, the only object of our study that does not derive its existence and meaning from its relationship to everything else. To understand ecology, therefore, indeed to understand anything, is to understand relationship, to understand process, both in space and in time. *Oikos*, our home, always comes with a spatial and a temporal direction. Ecology, therefore, is a study of our home, and goes a long way, though not all the way, to telling us who we are.

The centerpiece of religion is, similarly, a process which suggests relationship in time and in space. Religion derives from the Latin word *religio*, meaning, among other things, connectedness, bindedness, to origins, to roots, to that from which we have come. Ultimately, it is taken to mean relationship to Creator, to Divine Being, to God. It, too, obviously deals with who we are, who we might be. Like *oikos*, *religio* suggests vast breadth, the likelihood of limited human comprehension, and, as a result, a very natural sense of humility. It suggests not only mystery, mysticism, and that which we cannot fully understand, but it also suggests that we cannot be satisfied with not understanding because of our nature as thinking, reasoning beings. *Religio* also means binding, to be bound to, as in creator and created, to time and space. While *oikos* carries a great spatial character, it does not exclude temporal connectedness (connectedness of time). While *religio* includes somewhat greater temporal character, in Judaeo-Christian perception at least, it does not exclude spatial connectedness (connection in space). The two are part of one another and directly complement each other.

It is reason and scientific inquiry that takes us down the path of understanding our home, our *oikos*. It is faith that enables us to progress toward a sense (but not truly an understanding) of our origins, *religio*. Both searches are natural components to being human, and thus reason and faith will always have their place.

All people are believers. All human beings are people of faith. All people have religion, in one way or another. All people have values. And all people have spiritual experience, and therefore a spiritual side to their being. One may well ask, in what do people believe? In what do they place their faith. What is the nature of their religion? What are their values? But that all people have them, there is no doubt.

The answer to the questions on belief, faith, religion may relate to traditional questions of belief framed by the world's great religions. Or, they may focus more closely on our beliefs and assumptions about science, technology, the "techno-fix," about economics and growth for growth's sake, about consumption. It is very clear, for example, that some people's religious faith might be described as "shop 'til you drop." It might be described by the acquisition and consumption of "stuff," simply for the sake of such consumption.

And of our values it can be said that they are best defined as how we live in ordinary circumstances each hour and each day of our lives. Our values may well bear little relationship to what we might claim them to be (or perhaps might like them to be). We wear our values for the most part very publicly, available for all to see.

There is no question that our values and our religious or faith beliefs play a role in our attitudes toward sustainability and the way in which we would define sustainability. Further influencing our definition, our sense of meaning of this now vital concept of our future direction, is the reality that "unsustainability" has a negative connotation, placing great pressure on individuals and institutions to avoid that designation at all costs. This pressure creates the temptation to distort and trivialize any definition of the word. And, since change does not come easily for humans and is often surrounded by fear, we find ourselves witnessing far more cosmetic movement toward sustainability than real movement.

As reason and faith become congruent, as they flow together, what might be the result, and what might that result look like? Can one work without the other? Can true ecological thought and an ecological value system work without a sense of *religio*, a sense of faith, a sense of mystery, and the humility that that sense compels? Can *religio* work without reason, without questioning, without scientific inquiry in the best sense, without a denial of who we are? Can humans not think and still be fully human? Can sustainability work without underlying spiritual values, without *religio*, without faith? Or is the success of ecological sustainability effort inevitably connected to the development, practice, and nurturance of spiritual values? Are there practical models of sustainability and spirituality working together congruent with one another? It is the purpose of this study to answer this question and to investigate possible models of such practice, such as they are at the dawn of the twenty-first century. It is necessary, however, to first gain a greater and less reductionistic sense of what is meant by ecology and by sustainability, and also what is meant by spirituality. This necessity is particularly important in light of the great degree of reductionism that has already been applied to the idea of ecology, sustainability, spirituality and religion, and the distortion of these ideas which has resulted.

ECOLOGY AND RELIGION

It is tempting to measure real sustainability by its consonance with the principles of ecology, the latter principles appearing at this point in our evolution to represent the closest proximity to reality. It is encumbent upon us, therefore, to start off with a clear understanding of these principles, and, further, to conceptualize their very radical nature, as this nature suggests what might well be necessary for us to achieve sustainability.

Science and sustainability inevitably intersect in the principles and practice of ecology, the science of interrelationship, the study of home and context. They invariably intersect in the new science of conservation biology, especially with its strong values component. They intersect also in the sciences of restoration and remediation, the deliberate alteration for the better of already altered environments. And they intersect in the science of natural resource management, especially as the latter employs concepts of sustained yield, carrying capacity, demography, and limits. But nowhere is the intersection of science and sustainability more prescient, more immediate, more fundamental than in the area of enchantment, of the awe-inspiring impact of the unknown, of the newly discovered, and of the sacrality, the respect, the reverence, the awe, and the humility engendered by the power of discovery. In our time, we have not lacked such demonstration.

Ecology, as we have seen, means study of the home. The environment overall, at least at the scale of the planetary system, planet Earth, is taken as home, though some would even argue for the cosmos more broadly. It is the study of the home, spatially and temporally, in space and in time, and accepts the observer, the student of the home, to be a part of (and not separate and apart from) that home, an entity inclusive, not exclusive. Ecological thought is the philosophy of ecology, the conceptualization of the idea of ecology, the ways of understanding ecology, in the minds of humans.

Ecology is very often interpreted more narrowly and more reductionistically, as a science and not as an art, and as a division of biological science. Although ecology is fundamentally wholistic and cannot truly be reduced, the reductionistic culture in which it resides has in fact subdivided and reduced ecology into many parts, including animal ecology, plant ecology, forest ecology, insect ecology, marine ecology, soil ecology, and so forth. Human ecology infrequently appears as a subdivision and, when it does, it usually replaces what once was called "home economics" and focuses on the human's relationship to the built environment, to clothing and fashion, to food, and to other elements of one's immediate surroundings.

The principles of ecology can be summarized, as Barry Commoner said a long time ago, as everything is connected to, is a part of, every other thing. Nature knows best. Everything must go somewhere. There is no such thing as a free lunch.

These principles of ecology are perhaps the best way to approach a true and comprehensive meaning of the word.[1]

1.   Every thing is connected to, related to, interconnected to, and interrelated with, every other thing. Everything is a part of everything else, not only spatially but temporally as well. Everything is implicated in everything else. We are situated in an implicate order, and thus everything is a microcosm of all other things. We and all things are embedded in a context, within the universe. As Thomas Berry says, being within the phenomenal order, the universe itself is the only text without a context. This is always expressed as the first and most significant principle of ecology, and yet few persons and nearly no institutions in our society behave as if they believe it. It is so opposed in principle to our dominant world view and thus to the entire organization of modern society that it simply might be too much for most people to accept in practice. And yet, curiously, it is never questioned as the first expressed principle of ecology.

2.   Nature knows best is often expressed as the second principle of ecology. This can be misleading, for "nature" is commonly taken in our world view to mean something outside of and apart from us. But, in ecological thought, the word "nature" is fully inclusive of all humanity. (As the American expressionist artist Jackson Pollock once remarked upon being advised to focus more on nature in his work, "I am nature." He was absolutely right.) "Nature knows best" thereby takes on a different connotation and does not constitute some form of nature worship. Thomas Berry and others increasingly tell us of

nature's revelatory character, that nature stands with scripture in Judaeo-Christianity as a source of revelation of the Divine. To model our behavior after the way and patterns of nature, and not fight nature, and falsely believe we can conquer nature (which is, in effect, to conquer ourselves) is what ecological principle requires.

3. Everything must go somewhere. What goes around, comes around. There is no such place as "away." If you think you threw it away, you likely threw it in someone else's backyard (or succeeding generations' backyards). There is no such thing as waste. Everything has a role, has a job to do, in effect fits in. We desperately wish to believe otherwise, and do not want to dwell on our "waste" as returning to haunt us. We are less concerned about the haunting of future generations.

4. There is no such thing as a free lunch. Again, we very much want to believe otherwise. Any attitude that supports taking advantage of some other person, of the natural ecosystem, or of future generations violates ecological principle and imposes a cost. There are no bargains. All totals up (which is not only an ecological but also a Christian principle, a view of the Last Judgment). We very much want to believe we can get a bargain, but there are no bargains.

To recognize these principles, and to do so in ordinary everyday life, is to understand it is possible to think ecologically, to be governed daily by an ecological mindset or frame of reference. But to think ecologically is to resist, to resist the common culture and much of the system of society around us. It is to be countercultural, not unlike the degree of counterculture required by faith belief, required by religious thought, more specifically by Christianity and others of the world's religions. This is especially the case if we accept the broad cosmologic ecological belief of Thomas Berry, theologically adept ecologian, geologian, ethicist, celebrant of science and the spirit, celebrant of ecology, cosmology, quantum physics, Einsteinian relativity, some say "earth saint," and whose thought lies implicitly if not always explicitly at the very heart of those whose work is the subject of this study.

Environmental ethics dictates that the concept of stewardship, of land, of ecosystems, and so forth, is insufficient. Sacramentality, the concept of sacrality of earth, of creation, is a necessary component of environmental ethics, acknowledging as it does that, while distinct, we are not unconnected to the environment. (Within Christianity, even Benedictine stewardship, so highly regarded and important, is incomplete without sacramentality.) Aldo Leopold's environmental ethic includes sacramentality, a sense of the sacred—one need only to look at his famous passages on the green eyes of the dying wolf to understand that.[2]

We have now determined that the environment is a religious question, a question of moral choice and spiritual values, and that it is a religious question more fundamentally than it is a scientific, economic, or political question. Hence, we must accept that its resolution will be found within the religious or spiritual realm. Such resolution will be found, will come, as a by-product of:

- a strong sense of place
- the conscious development of a sense of connectedness with nature and of the cultivation of a sense of awe and wonder
- honest humility in the face of the cosmos
- a knowledge of and appreciation for the basic principles of ecology (and, most importantly, the foremost principle: everything is connected to everything else)
- an appreciation of wholeness and the implicate order of all phenomena
- a sense of the sacred and a feeling of reverence which normally comes with that sense
- a sense of the Creator within the created, of God in all
- for the Christian, an acceptance of the humanity of Christ and not just the divinity
- an understanding and an acceptance of right livelihood through the principle of swideshi (Hindu, Jain), through the principles elucidated in the Eight-fold Noble Path (Buddhist), through the principle of subsidiarity (Christian)

If these tenets are accepted, then how might we translate them to achieve sustainability of our lives, our humanity, our spirituality, our ecosystem of which we are a part and upon which we are dependent?

ON LIVING SUSTAINABLY

The concept of sustainability, of sustainable living, of how to live in such a manner that individuals, families, society as a whole might be sustained indefinitely into the future is on the minds of many people and is reflected in the agendas of many institutions. This can only be so because there is a real or implied threat to our sustainability as long as we continue on the path we have been pursuing in modern times, and especially in the post-World War II era. People know or suspect, almost innately, that our societal and perhaps even our species continuity is threatened if we continue to carry on as we do.

These deep-seated and disquieting feelings are leading to a great deal of attention to sustainable development, sustainable agriculture, sustainable living. And the word "sustainability" is being so widely used to refer to so many different things as to become meaningless, to distort, and to confuse.

The meaning of "sustainability," as commonly used, becomes more shallow, more superficial with the passage of each year. Why more superficial? Because true sustainability is exceedingly difficult to achieve without making basic changes in our values and in our lifestyle which we really do not want to make. For example, as mentioned, can a sustainable society exist dependent upon enormous usage of nonrenewable and ecologically damaging fossil fuel? We are nearly a totally fossil fuel-based society—it underlies all that we do, indeed, it even represents how we define ourselves as a people in modern times. And yet, on the ground of nonrenewability alone, fossil-fuel dependency (at any level) is counter to any reasonable interpretation of sustainability—it is inherently unsustainable. When one adds the enormous ecological by-product cost, not the least of which is likely climate change and holes in the Earth's protective ozone layer, fossil-fuel dependency becomes even that much less sustainable.

Given that a shift away from fossil fuel dependency will be nothing less than traumatic for the continuing functioning of our modern and particularly our American society, we are most reluctant and exceedingly poorly equipped to simply become sustainable, to carry out those tasks which would either make us sustainable or at least improve our sustainability ratio.

The true task, the true challenge of achieving sustainability which lies before us is most certainly not going to become achievable without something more than reliance on reason, on rationality, on science, or on secular ethics and values. The task of shifting mainstream thought and behavior is just too formidable. There is most assuredly going to need to be reliance on something additional, on some form of deep-seated faith, perhaps on some sort of spirituality, or some sort of religion, religion defined broadly, not narrowly, which will strengthen humans sufficiently to face the challenge implied in making changes which must increasingly be viewed as necessary. And this faith must be buttressed with the strength that comes from community, from communal support of one type or another. Reassurance needs to be given that we do not face alone such a basic and formidable challenge, the challenge of going forward with a basic change in our value system, the challenge of stepping off into the unknown, into the unfamiliar. Hence, it may well be that "faith communities" or "communities of faith" will need to form to assist society, a society so often made up of collections of individuals who are trained to see and to think individually rather than communally or collectively.

If such faith communities are needed, where does one look for models? Imperfect models are not uncommon. Perfect models are not to be found—flaws are all too common in each of us individually and in all of us collectively. But imperfect models do exist and are available for study.

The indigenous peoples of the planet, indigenous cultures and traditions are available for study, though few pure such cultures continue to exist—reliance must therefore be placed on historians and anthropologists for guidance. Heartening from a sustainability viewpoint, regardless of how much or how little we seem to know of such people, is the apparent universality of ecological and spiritual viewpoint held by these peoples over the ages, notwithstanding differences of continent, climate, or any other physical or cultural differences which may characterize them. They have a universality, a universal eco-spirituality which is profound, an ecological and spiritual value system which is eminently worthy of further investigation.

Perhaps among the few successful examples of communities actually living by ecological principles, in deed as well as in word, in practice as well as in theory, is the aforementioned indigenous peoples of the world (more so historically than at present). But there are other examples of modern communities one might cite. A contemporary American example is that of American women religious, some of whom are following the inspiration of geologian Thomas Berry (who, in fact, takes some of his own inspiration from indigenous peoples, particularly from North America).

As there are principles of ecology, so also there are principles of sustainability. Undoubtedly, there are many sets of principles of sustainability, not the least of which emanates from religious doctrine, such as the Sermon on the Mount. However, I believe there is particular value, and ecologically sensitive value, to be found in Wendell Berry's seventeen principles from his essay "Conserving Communities"; and, from Helen and Scott Nearing's *Guiding Principles for a Good Life*. All three of these philosopher practitioners are deeply ecological in their approach.

Principles of sustainability in human affairs can be identified at the community level and at the level of the individual. The focus of Wendell Berry's writing has been the role of the individual in community, so the seventeen principles of sustainability which Wendell Berry put forth in his book *Another Turn of the Crank* are fundamentally communal in nature, and, in all his principles, community is at the center. From supplying local needs first, to questioning "labor-saving," (which often means the loss of local work) to community self-investment, the use of "local currency," the connectedness of urban places with their rural hinterland, to a cooperative rather than a competitive economy, Wendell Berry provides a strong, practical, and community-based guide to sustainability.[3] Wendell Berry remains an important and enduring source of insight and inspiration to many of the communities mentioned in this volume. One can find a high degree of coherence between each of Berry's points and the practice of most of the communities described in this volume.

On ecological sustainability from an individual perspective, Helen and Scott Nearing have much to offer. In their *Guiding Principles for a Good Life*, they posit: unity and wholeness; the life of the mind and the spirit; the importance of association with fellow citizens; self-communion; harmony with the Earth; simplicity and right livelihood; taking joy in workmanship; mutual aid and harmlessness; and purposeful living. A compilation of the values the Nearings represented would include the following from their teachings:

Do the best you can, whatever arises.
Be at peace with yourself.
Find a job you enjoy.
Live in simple conditions; housing, food, clothing; get rid of clutter.
Contact nature every day; feel the earth under your feet.

Take physical exercise through hard work; through gardening or
  walking.
Don't worry; live one day at a time.
Share something every day with someone else; if you live alone,
  write someone; give something away; help someone else.
Take time to wonder at life and the world; see some humor in life
  where you can.
Observe the one life in all things.
Be kind to the creatures.
Simplify and order life;
Plan ahead;
Follow the line resolutely;
Eliminate nonessential things;
Keep distractions to a minimum;
Live day by day, by bread labor, with nature, with people,
  establishing worthwhile contacts;
Collect and organize material (that provides an important record
  or substantiates ideas);
Do research and follow trends;
Write, lecture, and teach;
Keep in close contact with the class struggle (social justice);
Acquire an understanding of basic and cosmic forces, gradually
  uniting together a unified, integrated, poised personality that is
  constantly learning and growing.[4]

I am not aware of any connection made by any of the communities
discussed in this book to the work or thought of Helen or Scott Nearing,
agnostics in their belief. And yet, an understanding of the principles put
forth and modeled by the Nearings in their lives goes far to aid in understanding the spiritual community models discussed herein.

On the question of sustainability, there appears to be no question
that we cannot sustain our present lifestyle and energy consumption patterns unless we are talking of an ever-decreasing few of us sustaining this
level at the expense of the many, of increasing numbers falling by the
wayside. The question is increasingly whether we can sustain a modicum
of human life at a reasonable modern societal level given the deteriora-
tion of the ecosystem upon which we depend. Phrases such as sustainable growth and sustainable development are also used to describe this
phenomenon. If growth is here used in the usual way, that is, a growing
and expandable economy, then sustainable growth is an oxymoron.

`Infinite growth in a finite environment is an absurdity. Sustainable development, on the other hand, is a useful concept as long as we accept the notion of development in the qualitative rather than just the quantitative sense. Development means change, but is not necessarily unidirectional: it can mean reduction in paving over the planet, restoration of the ecosystem, and qualitative improvement in human fulfillment rather than just the narrow notion of ever-increasing human impact and exploitation. "Sustainable living," to live sustainably, might well be the most meaningful phraseology.

To live sustainably is to live within the basic principles of ecology, in the face of a world living (and seemingly determined to live) unecologically, indeed, antiecologically. To live ecologically is to eliminate the concept of waste (for everything goes somewhere and plays some role); to understand that whatever hurts humanity as a whole or the system upon which we're dependent hurts us (for all is connected); to accept that there is no such thing as a "bargain" and that we should not spend our lives searching for same, or seeking to avoid paying our fair share (for there's no such thing as a free lunch); and to recognize and reverence nature for what nature is (namely, our teacher, for nature knows best). To live outside these rules is to court disaster, for nature will insure we pay, one way or another. Balance will prevail. Sustainability is not guaranteed. Since we are currently living outside these principles, we are living un- (or even anti-) ecologically, anti-integrally. Sustainability must come out of integrity. Our sustainability is, therefore, increasingly doubtful.

The study of ecological and biological linkages is a humbling experience, for it quickly gives insight into the enormous complexity of the way the system works. Such study soon uncovers the fact that the possibilities, the complexity of linkages and relationship, is well beyond the pale of human comprehension and most certainly will remain so. We know, and can know, so much less than we think we know. Geological possibilities, linkages, complexities are equally beyond our comprehension, in spite of the relative stability and rigidity our mind normally assigns to the physical structure of the Earth and its forms. A visit to any of America's great western geological parks and landscapes should humble us as to the incomprehensible possibilities of possible earth features and composition, if we but reflect upon it. These possibilities, likewise, have no known limit which we can ascertain.

We cannot under any circumstances claim or assume power over the Earth, the global ecosystem, for what we know or can claim to know is as nothing. We can only wonder, appreciate, be grateful for the beauty and the fascination of complexity, and yield or surrender to that which is greater than we are, a perfect depiction of the thought and way of life of the models of sustainability described in this volume.

In order to create a vision of what might be a relatively ideal and successful linkage of ecology and spirituality, the following chapter details what this author considers to be particularly strong success stories as models of sustainability, spiritually based.

Chapter Three

OUTSTANDING MODELS
OF SUSTAINABILITY

If one found an example of true ecological sustainability, how would one recognize it? How would one know? By any rational, reasonable set of criteria, real examples of ecological sustainability are rare. In contrast, current existing models of sustainability often address one or a few areas of life (e.g., energy). There are very few examples which give a full picture.

I have found five such particularly strong models of ecological sustainability in my research: one on the high plains of North Dakota, one in the desert of southern New Mexico, one on the prairie of Nebraska, and two in the midwestern farm country of Iowa and Indiana. What the monastics of Sacred Heart Monastery in North Dakota, the Sisters of multiple religious orders and lay people of Tierra Madre in New Mexico, the Dominican Sisters of Heartland Farm in Kansas, and the Franciscan Sisters of Michaela Farm in Indiana, and Prairiewoods in Iowa hold in common is substantial and comprehensive progress on the road to ecological sustainability. It is deeply embedded in their spirituality and sustainable in their lives and in those whom they inspire. All five examples focus on the integration of spirituality and ecological principle and all five continually and significantly walk their talk. If we are going to learn anything from actual, real-world models, these are strong candidates as teachers. There may well be other such candidates across the land unknown to me, but these would likely equate to the best of them. Many other models mentioned in this volume have one or more true success stories to convey, from which we can learn. However, most such models have not achieved the higher level of integration of spiritual values with ecological values which brings the depth, passion and drive to sustain what would otherwise surrender to the pressure of an unsustainable culture. One of the serious, common problems encountered in this research has been the unsustainability of sustainability projects, and related efforts. It is the depth of spirituality and not the mere presence (or rationality) of ecological principle which must be present to sustain them in the face of superior forces seeking their demise.

An important way of gaining an understanding of the amorphous and elusive meaning of the word "sustainability" is to draw a picture from real-world examples, of what one might truly mean by the word "sustainable." It is the purpose of this chapter to do just that. Likewise, it is the purpose of this chapter, to broaden the subject from focus on merely the community itself, its structure and organization, to the broader context in which it is embedded. There is no suggestion here that local sustainability can exist as a limited practice in isolation from the broader world in which it is embedded; we need to consider each community's relationship with that broader world.

In considering these communities, it is important to note that, in North American society, it is Roman Catholics who have traditionally formed spiritual communities. It is also true, however, that the influence of other spiritualities is strong, in that these eco-spiritual groups are highly ecumenical and even interfaith in nature, and their work is shared with visitors, even a majority of visitors, from non-Catholic traditions. Interest in interdenominational Judaeo-Christian spirituality, Eastern philosophy, and indigenous peoples' spirituality is strong.

MONKS FACE THE WIND

Sacred Heart Monastery in Richardton, North Dakota is an outstanding example of spiritually based sustainability. The dramatic story Sacred Heart presents relates to wind energy, but this alone could not qualify the monastery for such an esteemed status of outstanding community model. How the monks use their land, obtain their food, live daily, and integrate their land-based ecological approach with their Christian spirituality, their Benedictine charism, is a critical part of the broader whole. Their Benedictine monastic approach is further explored in a chapter on that subject—it is their specific value as a sustainability model, their action rather than their contemplation, which is of interest here.[1]

North Dakota is an important coal state. The state has vast reserves of lignite coal economically available through relatively inexpensive but ecologically damaging surface mining (strip mining), combined with a rail-based transport infrastructure to transport the coal to nearby power plants. The low Btu (heat energy) content of this soft lignite coal economically necessitates location of the electric power plants near the mine-mouth, near the source of the coal. Hence, North Dakota has invested mightily in large-scale electric power plants and coal gasification plants in the western part of the state, at great cost to air quality. Large amounts of highly polluting, high sulfur-content coal produces a proportionately small amount of energy. The picture we have is that of a highly invested, coal energy producing state (with a declining agricultural economy, leading to an economically troubled state which is dramatically losing population); and a state with a high tolerance for environmental pollution, pollution not only damaging to itself but also contributing to long-distance air pollution and climate change/greenhouse warming as well.

Enter the women of Sacred Heart Monastery in the rural heartland of western North Dakota coal country. These monks interpret their Benedictine spirituality as necessitating an ecological lifestyle. Their goal is a lifestyle that is as ecological as they can possibly make it, recognizing that how they live in North Dakota affects areas far from North Dakota through global climate change and global environmental pollution. Conscious of their choices, their response is serious and determined: to produce their own energy from renewable, local and non-fossil fuel sources. They position themselves so that after providing for all their own needs, they make nonpolluting energy available to others. Realizing that North Dakota is the single windiest state in the nation, wind turbines are obviously the method to use. Recognizing that the Danes are now the world leaders in wind energy technology and that California is the likeliest United States source for parts and equipment, the monks, following upon thorough research, strike out to bring in, first one and then a second wind turbine, producing about 60 percent of their own electricity needs in 2000. (Their goal is 100 percent plus, meaning they are preparing to sell some to the community, including another monastery nearby, as well as the local townspeople). The battle with local and state government and with electric utility companies to over-come countless bureaucratic obstacles in this coal-dominated state was itself a Herculean task, but the monks persisted (as they have in many ways for sixteen hundred years), and their two wind turbines are plainly visible today from the only interstate highway in their region. Deter-mined to be of help to others, they have created a wind energy website which is now teaching people all over the world that they, too, can move in this direction, and precisely how to do so.

According to Sr. Paula Larson, O.S.B., former prioress of Sacred Heart Monastery, the Benedictine monks here had developed over many years an interest in ecology, both through their personal education and through some activism as members of environmental organizations. Thus, when the opportunity for wind energy development and other eco-logical initiatives presented themselves at the monastery, the community support came rapidly. With respect to the wind turbines, it took two years from the point of decision to go this route to the operationalization of the turbines. Sr. Paula says, however, that since the learning curve is now be-hind them, additional turbines could be made operational in three months. The earlier development involved many meetings with the utility and the utility was not very supportive of the project, unlike state gov-ernment which was very supportive and provided a small grant. The util-ity required paperwork ranging from an initial letter of intent, approval of an electric connection plan, acquiescence to a set of written require-ments, and a legal agreement prior to going on line. Sr. Paula reports that today: "As to the utility, the climate is much different now, much more positive. Times have changed and other consumers are interested in green power so over the last year the utility has visited with us about being a potential provider to them of green power in the future."[2] This is a re-markable reversal, indeed, in this coal-dominated state. It is likely that the monks of Sacred Heart Monastery are at least partly responsible for the change of attitude in North Dakota.

Exemplative of the debate conducted by the monks with local au-thorities seeking to put obstacles in their way is the story of one govern-ment official who told them that they could not proceed without first conducting a scientific study to determine if there was sufficient wind. Upon which the prioress of the monastery simply took the bureaucrat outside and held up her finger to test the wind, blowing that day as most days, in this, the windiest state in the nation! She made her point and a $10,000 study was averted. (Of course, scientifically speaking, one day proves nothing, but one need only turn to long-standing U.S. Weather Service data to understand the frequency, velocity, and direction of the wind, on average, year-round, in that place, proving the nonsensical nature of any requirement to conduct an expensive and time-consuming study to determine if there will be enough wind. It is also important to realize that the stated requirement to conduct such a study is not likely directed at acquiring needed scientific information as it is meant to be an impediment to deter the project, delay the project, or frustrate the people involved, a most questionable motive.)

If the persistence, determination, hard work, and success of the wind energy project were the whole story at Sacred Heart Monastery, then this monastery would not be a candidate for the comprehensive model of sustainability which it is. (The linkage of this local and global concern for energy and for one's own energy impact must, therefore, be linked to broader aspects of the monk's daily lifestyle and interrelationship with the land.) The monastery's own experience with these obstacles placed in their path has led the monks to become wind energy activists in North Dakota, trying to get the state to remove obstacles to conversion to wind energy for themselves and other North Dakotans who would move in this direction.

The late Sr. Bernadette Bodine of this community wrote: "There is a natural tie between us as Sacred Heart Benedictines and the development of wind energy. We are here for the long haul. That is part of our vow of stability. . . . This sense of place and commitment of a group of people for life helps us to dig in our roots, and to nourish and care for the earth where we are."[3] According to Prioress Sr. Paula Larson: "We started into the wind turbine project for two reasons. First, we had uncontrollable utility bills which continued to rise and we could determine no other way to control the cost. Second, the environment is a precious gift of God and we wanted to see how much our small contributions could impact the poisonous gases (SO_2 and NO_x) that we sent into our breathing air. Also the (wind) turbines prevented carbon dioxide from going into the environment which is related to global warming."[4] In linking to her Benedictine charism, Prioress Larson comments: "On the day we blessed our turbines, we had the following on the program cover, and we feel it sums up our attitude and disposition to this adventure with God's created wind:

Nothing is clear-cut when we choose to follow You.
We need a spirit of openness
A spirit of trust
A spirit of adventure
The Holy Spirit is your gift to us
The spirit of openness
The spirit of trust
The spirit of adventure.[5]

The linkage of this local and global concern for energy and for one's own energy impact was, therefore, linked to broader aspects of the monks' daily lifestyle and interrelationship with the land.

Take llamas, for instance. Yes, llamas. The monks of Sacred Heart have been raising and breeding llamas for nearly a decade. They maintain a herd of fifteen to twenty at any one time; they breed them for the sale of offspring (providing very good income); pasture them on their own pasture, and winter feed them on the monastery's hay crop; use them as a control over invasive plants (they eat spurge, a major problem plant in the West); use the llamas excrement as fertilizer (the only fertilizer used on their grounds); package that excrement and market it for further income; use the llamas for animal control, keeping deer out of the vegetable gardens; spin the wool and produce both raw wool and a finished product (felt hats, for which they are known); and, very importantly for their spirituality and spiritual practice, engage in spinning to enhance contemplation and, in fact, provide to the public spinning meditation workshops, very much in the spirit of Mahatma Gandhi, who was an important advocate of this technique of meditation. All this from llamas! (And if the monks chose to keep sheep, llamas would provide high quality predator control as well.)

With wind energy and llamas we still have not fully explored Sacred Heart as a sustainability model. As with most monastic communities, Sacred Heart maintains sizeable gardens (protected from the ravages of deer by llamas, a fact which enables big gardens in this country). These gardens are operated organically, using no chemicals and no chemical fertilizer, only llama manure and compost. They produce mixed vegetables and supply all of the annual potato and asparagus needs for the community (which consists of twenty-four permanent monks and numerous short-term visitors year-round). Additionally, chokecherries and juneberries produce berries and serve as windbreaks. They believe in some level of food independence, as per the Rule of Benedict under which they operate.

Overall, the Benedictine monks of Sacred Heart are strong ecological thinkers and routinely connect wind energy, gardens, and food supply to llamas, fertilizer, spinning, meditation, and to wool production. Organic agricultural approaches come naturally (Why would we use chemicals? they ask). So also is their approach to energy conservation, good use of passive solar as well as wind energy, as much to remove themselves from connection to air pollution and global environmental problems as to save money or achieve independence (although both of the latter are valued). They do not develop long-term planning, living by the day and season, but are clearly committed to a path of increased ecological practice and sustainability. They are one community and act as a group: if you lose money, you lose everybody's money, and there is no one else to supply money. They have great reverence for the earth, and have some ecologically based liturgies. They have good connections to the broader community, especially to small farmers and ranchers for whose plight they have great sensitivity. As would be expected, they have a strong world view patterned by Benedictine monastic spirituality. They are strong on art, its importance and its power. They have their own strong ecological ethic, not especially patterned after anyone else. Blessed with good leadership, they are strongly non-hierarchical, much in keeping with other ecologically oriented communities. The idea of independence and self-sufficiency to the greatest extent possible is critical to the whole sustainability/spirituality notion, as it is to Sacred Heart Monastery. Such is needed so that we are able to accept our moral responsibilities and have true freedom. Thus, wind power on farms (or monasteries) to provide the needed electrical energy is important, as is reduction in market dependency (and especially international market dependency), and market (i.e., external) control. One might conclude from this that Benedictine spirituality (and Catholic social teaching and Christian gospel precept) require cessation of the way in which we live, in terms of energy and ecology, so that we must actively seek and practice alternatives.

Since Sacred Heart monastery is a monastic community, the reader is referred to the chapter on Benedictine monasticism and ecology for greater insight into the forces underlying the behavior and practice of these western North Dakota monks who are among the few people in our society showing a strong path toward sustainability and, through their charism and their honesty, is leading the people of the coal state of North Dakota on a very different path.

STRAWBALE IN THE DESERT

Most people, and particularly Catholics, would be surprised to learn that the largest strawbale housing development in the United States is being carried out by the Catholic Church. This is a project in southern New Mexico adjacent to the Mexican border and the Texas state line near El Paso and involves a planned community of no less than forty-seven strawbale solar houses each 1,500 sq. ft. in size, together with additional construction of a strawbale community center/library and office building, associated gardens, and public community recreational space filled with appropriate furnishings. All of this is on twenty acres.[6]

Why strawbale? Strawbale building construction is one of the most socially and ecologically just forms of architecture. It is socially just because it is so available to all kinds of people in need of housing, due to its very small expense and simple construction which unskilled people can readily master with guidance and direction. Socially just also because of the very little money needed for heating, cooling, or any form of care, relative to conventional housing. And ecologically just for the obvious reason that it is so highly insulated naturally that it requires very little fossil fuel burning for either heating or cooling at any season of the year. Strawbale homes at Tierra Madre community in New Mexico have "r" values (a measure of insulation) of forty-five in the walls and thirty in the ceilings. These very high insulation values, especially when complemented with passive solar energy, mean, in high altitude southern New Mexico, no heating in winter, and no air conditioning in summer, in spite of very cold winter nights and hot desert summer temperatures. To obtain this benefit, the thickness of the walls is measured in feet, the ceiling also, in fact, the width of hay bales. This means window sills which are actually window benches, for all windows are wide enough to sit in, not unlike the windows of medieval European castles. And the straw, covered over and sealed with three coats of stucco (adobe), lends itself to beautiful rounding and sculpting design effects not achievable with wood and other conventional building forms, contributing grace and beauty to these structures. Double-paned (thermal-paned) windows, heat-absorbing and slowly heat-releasing thermal tiles, passive solar design, solar hot water

heaters all enhance the eco-justice nature of these houses and this community. A serious look at wind turbines, composting toilets, and a desire
to get off the electrical grid and achieve electricity independence help
round out the picture here.

A further external portion of the Tierra Madre scene is the provision of a great amount of public spaces, with measures taken to assure
its maintenance and care indefinitely, a serious effort at permaculture[7]
(they're doing it, not just talking about it), and sizable community gardens to provide food, flowers, outdoor recreation, and nourishment for
the soul rounds out the picture. Irrigation support for the gardens is being
arranged by full gray water and gutter water containment from each
house. A complete natural history inventory of the site is now ongoing,
providing residents a clear picture of where they are, a sense of place.

Principles in this project are three Catholic nuns representing three
different religious orders (Sisters of Charity, Franciscans, and Sisters of
Mercy), and the Catholic Diocese of Las Cruces and its Bishop, Ricardo
Ramirez. The cofounder is Sister of Charity Jean Miller, and the Project
Director is a retired federal (BLM) wildlife biologist, Jaime Provencio.
Another important collaborator is the state of New Mexico, for the entire Tierra Madre community is on state land, land leased from the state
for ninety-nine years, with an option to renew for another ninety-nine
years. (And a very enthusiastic supporter of Tierra Madre and its ability
to create value on state land where no value existed before is New Mexico State Commissioner of Public Lands Ray Powell, a statewide elected
public official.)

One might well ask at this point, what is going on here at Tierra
Madre, at Sunland Park, New Mexico? Sr. Jean Miller would say that
Tierra Madre is about linking an option for the poor with an option for
the Earth. Sr. Jean is among those who equate social justice and eco-justice as one and the same. There is a critical housing shortage in the greater
El Paso metropolitan area and strawbale construction with passive solar
and solar hot water are viewed as one answer. Easier said than done, and
Sr. Jean, paralleling the action of Sr. Paula Larson to the north in North
Dakota, took on the forces that said this could not be done, and, with
diligence and persistence, prevailed. A big hurdle over loans and financ-
ing for such unconventional construction was one of many such hurdles,
added on to building permits, and even an appropriate source for the

straw (ideally this would be a local source but there aren't such, so it must be trucked in from the San Luis Valley of Colorado).

Heifer Project International with its interests in assisting low-income people to achieve security and independence, traditionally through provision of livestock and increasingly through gardens, is also a collaborator. While no major investments in large animals are likely at Tierra Madre, chickens (for eggs and meat) and rabbits are a distinct possibility.

Plans are afoot for a large permanent community center in the future, all strawbale with composting toilets, and off the electric grid. Meanwhile, a small one the size of a home is being prepared for the near term. Indicative of the special place that public or community land and facilities and their care hold in the eyes of the leadership here, the playground was the very first thing designed and built, to demonstrate the importance of public space, in the face of a culture, our culture, which says that public space, public facilities, are not important, and in a culture which is, in fact, losing its ability to "be" public.

Started with initial planning about 1994, this project was expected to be completed in May 2003, with a certain percentage of the forty-seven houses constructed by February 2002 in order to eliminate a significant portion of the debt. Each house will sell for $47,000 with financing available, and may be resold in the future with 25 percent of the difference between appraisal at time of purchase and resale appraisal. Thus, there is a control against speculation. The land remains in state ownership.

Providing both financial and moral support, Franciscans, Sisters of Charity, Sisters of Mercy, Dominicans, and Catholic Dioceses all have a central part of their charism to care for the poor, to care for the least among us. Once the equation of this "option for the poor," as it has been called, has been made to the option for the Earth, once social justice and eco-justice are married, Tierra Madre and the nation's largest strawbale housing development can happen. This, indeed, has happened in southern New Mexico where justice for the Earth and justice for humanity are seen to require one another.

HEARTLAND FARM

As wind energy is the physical organizing principle and symbol for the ecologically grounded Sacred Heart monastery, and as strawbale housing is the physical organizing principle for the ecologically grounded and ecologically comprehensive Tierra Madre community in New Mexico, so also three outstanding ecologically grounded and, as well, ecologically comprehensive earth-based religious communities in the prairie heartland of America have their physical organizing principle and symbol: the equation of healing of earth, healing of body, healing of spirit as one and the same, within the context of ecological agriculture. Heartland Farm in Kansas, an ecumenical Dominican community, Prairiewoods in Iowa, and Michaela Farm in Indiana, the latter two both Franciscan ecumenical communities, are three of many such faith-based eco-communities, and outstanding examples presenting the nation with impressive models.

Heartland Farm near Pawnee Rock in central Kansas is the westernmost of a string of Dominican eco-communities described elsewhere in this volume, and one which has succeeded in more directions and in more ways than many of the others, and against formidable odds.[8] A collaboration of Catholic Sisters with a strong Mennonite presence, the two insuring solid Christian Gospel and social justice values, supported by a steady ecumenical stream of Protestant and some Catholic workers and volunteers has made for a forceful ecological presence in this area of the Great Plains.

Heartland Farm is owned by the Dominican Sisters of Great Bend (Kansas) and is officially part of the ministry of that order, giving the farm an official status and considerable security into the future. This is grain country and Heartland Farm produces its share of organically grown alfalfa, rather than chemically produced. But much else is also produced. Beyond three alfalfa fields, a visitor to Heartland Farm sees much which reveals the community's philosophy:

- a circle garden at the entrance built in the style of nearby Indian tribal peoples, demonstrating respect for those who've gone before, an openness to indigenous peoples' spirituality, and an appreciation of their ecological values

- a big barn for food drying, and tool and equipment storage, support for sustainable agriculture, and soon to be reroofed with solar shingles

- one acre mixed vegetable garden, intensive double dug with garlic a major garden crop—highly prized among serious vegetarians, among others

- solar-heated walk-in cold frames for starter seedlings

- new strawbale-constructed building for a community activities center and greenhouse, with a heating source of radiant heat coming from floor pipes embedded in a concrete floor designed to look like tile and wood

- organically certified grain fields

- ancient white ash trees, some over two hundred years old, the presettlement virgin woodland

- a hermitage retreat house in a quiet more remote spot on the property, constructed of strawbale, equipped with a compost toilet, and solar electricity for lights and fan, a building off the utility grid

- a medieval-inspired labyrinth just completed on a former pasture

- bees and honey product

- a large donated "recycled" older house moved to the site from off the property

- the presence of chickens and lots of fresh eggs, chickens raised outdoors (formerly free range but labor shortage challenges have eliminated free range or pasture chickens for the time being)

- collection of rain water from all roof tops in barrels

- presence of a number of volunteers and a few interns, including one provided annually by the Mennonite church

- the very possible future view of meat and dairy goats (now being seriously discussed but none at present)

The community consists of Catholic women religious of currently two orders (three nuns), a Mennonite family of five, and three volunteers, all living long-term on the site, plus a steady stream of other helpers and visitors. This group of women pioneered Community Supported Agriculture (CSA) in this region, the first CSA effort in Kansas, but, after encouraging others in this area to take up this task, they now direct the organic product of its gardens to a large institution, the Dominican Motherhouse in nearby Great Bend.

The Dominicans of Great Bend purchased Heartland Farm in late 1987, paying $65,000 for the eighty acres, the century-old farmhouses and six farm buildings. In the year prior to the purchase, the Dominican community had passed a resolution to be in solidarity with small farmers and to work for the care of the Earth. The late Sr. Betty Jean Goebel spearheaded the effort with strong community support.

The Sisters operated a CSA at the farm from 1993 to 1998, with twenty to twenty-five shareholders each year. However, the great annual turnover of shareholders and the farm's remote location in the country-side necessitated delivery to the shareholders (rather than shareholder pick-up at the farm). This, along with the loss of some money in the venture, did not bode well for its continuance. This is unlike the circumstance in many other similar earth-based communities. The shareholders' inability to come to the farm seriously compromised the community-building value of CSA which the Sisters sought.

In 1999 the opportunity arose to devote the farm to providing food for the Dominican Sisters Motherhouse just fourteen miles away, as well as to feed the Heartland Farm community itself. The Motherhouse consumes half of the farm's production. Granted that the Motherhouse is available as a market and is desirous of being such, Heartland Farm is more fortunate than many such communities in having such a guaranteed market. CSA has not yet caught on in central Kansas, with the Wichita metro area supporting the only one in the region, so this option may not be available to Heartland Farm for some years.

The highest priority of Heartland Farm and the central focus of the community is intentional, ecumenical community, with governance by consensus. Retreats, workshops, and so on, at the interface of ecology and religion, with a particularly strong interest in wholistic health, are characteristic, but only to the extent they do not disrupt the natural, daily routine of the community and its subsistence nature (a subsistence especially powerful when one realizes the community operates at an income level which is below taxation).

Their social justice values means a certain amount of time is spent off the farm working in various ministries (organizing against the death penalty, prison and state hospital ministries, hospital nursing, etc.). This gravitates somewhat against expanding subsistence agriculture activity. Nevertheless, any ecological assessment would award very high marks in all areas to Heartland Farm, including purchasing practice, energy, food, building design, land management, cleaning materials, all of which work is conducted with a high level of consciousness concerning strong ecological values. Community members are very much in synch with that ecological thought at the practical working level.

A deeper probing into Heartland Farm reveals plans not only for a solar energy-shingled large barn roof replacement, but also a designation of the large barn for containment of storage batteries for solar electricity; a significant interest in wind energy, particularly in the coupling of wind and solar, serious enough as to think of selling electricity back to the grid; a radiant heat energy project involving four zones beneath the floors of the large new building; the use of rainwater for the water needs of the new building, needs which includes sinks, showers, pottery facilities, and in topping off solar hot water heating in what otherwise is a closed system.

There also is the production of the community's own straw (organic oats) for the production of strawbale construction material; organic oats rotate between organic alfalfa crops. Land is also being set aside for native grass, including some designated under the federal CRP (Conservation Reserve Program), and plans are afoot to double the size of the farm with purchase of an additional eighty acres for raspberry and other crop production.

Intentional ecumenical community is the central idea at Heartland Farm, with serious food production for the occupants and, as well, for the Motherhouse. However, Heartland Farm's central work commitment is counseling and healing of body, mind, and spirit, through gardening, pottery-making, therapeutic massage, and art. An unstated but nevertheless extremely important aspect of the Heartland enterprise is the modeling of spiritually inspired practical ecological behavior in every aspect. The level of that demonstration, of that witness, is profoundly powerful.

PRAIRIEWOODS

To the east on the tall grass prairie of eastern Iowa can be found the Franciscan settlement of Prairiewoods. Appropriately named, with half prairie and half woodland acreage, Prairiewoods presents to the visitor as complete a representation of ecological philosophy put into both design and daily practice as one is likely to find anywhere. A current one acre prairie ecology restoration project at present will soon be expanded to multiple acres, for example, nature trails through prairie and woodland; a conscious effort to beat back and check invasive plant species; two strawbale-constructed hermitage apartments with solar electricity, solar radiant heat, highly energy efficient refrigerators and other appliances, solar energy application in all the buildings (including, not the least, a large trombe wall, a wall which collects the heat of the sun through glass and into brick and stone, with slow release into interior airspace—a major financial investment made only by those strongly committed to solar energy); serious wind direction and velocity research on-site in preparation for future wind turbines for electricity; and ecological concerns over every small detail, including cleaning products and toilet paper, a very detailed and rounded program.[9]

Prairiewoods opened its doors on July 5, 1996.

The Franciscan Sisters of Perpetual Adoration (FSPA) of LaCrosse, Wisconsin purchased this farmland in 1961 and rented it out for crop production until the 1980s, at which time it was retired to Conservation Reserve (CRP) land.

Sr. Betty Daugherty, FSPA, founder of Prairiewoods, determined, with the inspiration of Sr. Miriam Therese MacGillis and Thomas Berry, to begin a center on this land which would integrate spirituality and ecology. Sr. Betty presented a proposal to her order to begin such a center, a proposal which was approved at both the local and broader level. Other members of the order were invited to be part of the group that would plan, build, and operate this center. Financial support has been and still is provided by the Franciscan order.

Delving more deeply at Prairiewoods, one finds that "simplicity circles" (i.e., small groups striving to support each other in living simply, and in resisting the culture in doing so) are quite evident in their programming, as are "conscious living" groups. One finds a conscious desire to help people move away from a preoccupation with self and toward environmental and social questions at the community level. A labyrinth (for meditation) and a "cosmic walk" (to develop a realization of who we are and where we fit in the universe, in time and space) are both available and much used. One finds there are many volunteers present, and the community is very good at attracting them. (Juvenile offenders also come, assigned by the courts as part of doing public service.)

The Franciscans at Prairiewoods are very advanced in both their ecological thought and their action, albeit quiet and understated. Their ecological values include every detail and their spiritual and ecological values are well balanced. In describing their raison d'être as an important land-based center for healing, they see a striking similarity between their own approach and the long-standing Pueblo Indian early spring tradition of fast running as a means of giving energy back to the Earth. In our times, we are told by the Prairiewoods Franciscans there is increasing acknowledgment that the earth has healing abilities, healing qualities, for spiritual, mental, and physical healing, and that there is an increasing recognition of this by people at all levels today, including health care professionals, religious people, priests, nuns, and other religious. People seek out centers of healing and in this the Franciscan eco-spirituality center sees itself as directly paralleling Southwest Indian Pueblos and their traditions. The visitor might well reflect that the Franciscan tradition itself, in its undiluted and undistorted form, carries its own eco-spiritual tradition, now eight centuries old.

What makes Prairiewoods such a significant example of spiritually based ecological sustainability is its marriage of theory and praxis, of talk and action. Prairiewoods expresses its spirituality, inspired by Thomas Berry, through its vision statement:

- To be open to the Divine Presence within all members of the Earth Community

- To integrate the principles of the universe: interiority, diversity, and communion

- To reverence all of creation as sacred and revelatory of the Holy

- To embody a lifestyle that cares for the Earth and celebrates the human

- To extend hospitality to all

- To impact ecological consciousness

Prairiewoods' intended purpose is posed in three questions:

- How do we in our busy lives remain true to (and humbled by) the mystery, both within and without?

- How do we approach the major issues of our day: ecology, the roles of humans in today's world, the need for healing in our society?

- How do we deal with the questions of faith and meaning?

Prairiewoods states as its goals, among other things, working with persons and groups knowledgeable in environmental studies and developing programs that will attract larger groups to ecological programs; expanding the field of wholistic energy and nutrition; and modeling their ecological philosophy in their operating style.

Moving from theory to praxis, from talk to action, in a very concrete way, the community embodies a lifestyle that cares for the Earth and celebrates the human in a number of different ways.

- It is continually increasing dependence on locally grown food, (including by deciding on a designated percentage of food from their own garden and from other local sources; installing a functioning root cellar for winter food storage; developing menus to incorporate locally grown food; purchasing 90 percent of meat locally and from local sources; encouraging local community supported agriculture; obtaining 50 percent of storage crops from their own garden (garlic, onions, potatoes, squash); obtaining 30 percent of food overall from local Farmers Markets; drying and using teas from their own herb gardens; hosting workshops on making soups, breads, and the use of locally grown foods.

- It is researching and implementing alternative energy sources (wind energy, solar electric heat, hybrid gas/electric vehicle).

- It is using best practices for land/woods management (including tree and shrub planting, ecological development plans, erosion control, pollutant filtrations, periodic burning of prairie and savanna, creating tree groves for shade).

- It celebrates earth and humans through ritual, including a whole range of land-based activities.

- It lives lightly on Earth, including evaluation plans for assessing ecological consciousness in their operations.

- It offers programs on the work of Thomas Berry and like-minded eco-spiritual thinkers.

- It offers a range of programs that connect lifestyles with ecological concerns.

The ecological features that one might find today at Prairiewoods are many:

- In all buildings one finds non-toxic paint, nontoxic carpeting, mineral wool insulation (a natural material).

- In the Center Building one finds compact fluorescent lights in corridors (15 watt bulbs); natural lighting in most rooms; passive solar light and some heat in atrium; super insulation throughout the building (mineral wool); double pane windows with argon gas in between the panes; windows that open so as to get natural air conditioning; eight energy efficient furnaces and eight air conditioners (zoned)—so that only those being used need to be turned on; double doors at entrances to catch cold air or hot humid air before it enters the building; berming around some walls—extra insulation, which maintains constant temperature in winter and summer.

- In the Guest House one finds hot water for showers and other uses provided by solar panels; berming around entire building—maintains cool temperature in summer and warm temperature in winter (around 55 degrees); windows that open and ceiling fans in all rooms, instead of air conditioning.

- In the Residence (three apartments) one finds a trombe wall (a wall that has brick on the inside and glass on the outside—sun penetrates glass to heat brick which in turn heats two apartments on any day that the sun shines; because of the position of the sun in summertime, that is, more directly overhead, the wall does not heat in summer); sunspace in third apartment; fans pull hot air out in the summer and pull sun heat into the apartments in the winter.

Ecological practices conducted at Prairiewoods include the use of:

- reusable dishes, flatware, and many kitchen items (eclectic look)
- washable cups and napkins—elimination of all styrofoam products and paper products in food service
- some recycled furniture
- cloth napkins, instead of paper
- recycled paper products (office and cleaning)
- the second side of paper for computers and when photocopying
- the recycling of all cardboard, chipboard, glass, paper, plastic, tins, and so forth
- nontoxic materials for cleaning

- compost from all biodegradable materials from kitchen
- vegetarian meals whenever possible—eating lower on the food chain.

In witnessing this evolution from eco-philosophical expression to very specific eco-practices, which are actually in operation—they "walk their talk"—shows clearly why this Franciscan community of Prairiewoods would qualify as a prime example of spiritually grounded sustainability. And while they themselves clearly "walk their talk," they are equally adept at helping others outside their community with a well-developed Environmental Outreach Program, with a Food and Faith Program, a Voluntary Simplicity Program, a Lawn Stewardship Program (which recognizes the particularly grave ecological problem of chemically maintained church and other lawns), and an Energy Star Congregations Program which provides practical assistance to achieve energy conservation.

Prairiewoods provides a sterling example of an ecological and Franciscan spirituality at work. Indiana's Michaela Farm presents to us another Franciscan example of true sustainability at work.

MICHAELA FARM

With respect to the teachings of Thomas Berry, it has been said of the Oldenburg Franciscans who operate Michaela Farm near Oldenburg in southeastern Indiana, that they don't teach it, they live it.[10] Going for the highest form of organic farm certification obtainable, Demeter (biodynamic) certification, is indicative of this action. On their farmland, one also finds a strong Community Supported Agriculture (CSA) operation, and rotational grazing in the pastures as well. A basic nutrient input to this farm operation is the composting of the food waste of both the high school and the Franciscan Sisters Motherhouse which is on the property. (Less successful has been the effort to market organic farm product to the Motherhouse—the aging population of nuns is just not culturally attuned in this direction. This is unfortunate since organic farm products are not only delicious but healthy.)

Active farming ceased at the Franciscan Motherhouse in 1987, with the land leased to local farmers. It was in 1991 that the new effort,

Michaela Farm, was born. The vision for Michaela Farm to become the model sustainable community of today was initiated by the General Council (leadership team) of the Franciscans from 1990 to 1994 and approved by the congregation in that period.

Michaela Farm's internship program was started in 1995 and has averaged two to six interns at any one time, each serving from three months to two years. Sr. Ann Marie Quinn, codirector of Michaela Farm, remarks that "Everyone that comes has their own gifts that they bring. Some have experience with livestock and want experience with organic gardening, and vice versa. Others have no experience in agriculture, but are concerned about food issues and want to learn more. Still others have a dream of being sustainable and homesteading on their own. Hopefully, we're able to capitalize on the gifts of each and help them in their growth process."[11]

In a recent development, Michaela Farm has received a grant to put in a pond, for biodiversity on the land and for irrigation supply for the farm. The sisters are now considering the possibility of aqua-farming.

Michaela Farm has regular student interns full time in an organized internship program, as well as the help of two neighboring farmer couples who believe in the project. There is a high level of staff organization and planning here, and the Farm is committed not only to the thinking of Thomas Berry, but also to the new homeopathic biodynamic farming approaches coming from the biodynamic farming programs in this country and overseas. Michaela Farm's effort is sufficiently impressive in this local agricultural area that farm neighbors, including those in neighboring counties, are being influenced by the model approach of these Franciscans. The program is also extremely ecumenical in its on-site staff, its interns, and those many visitors who come to the farm to participate and learn. It is at Michaela Farm and places like it that one can begin to envision the new role of such spiritually driven ecologically sustainable farms as teachers of the community, as teachers of one another, and even as replacements for public entities such as the Cooperative Extension Service, given that Michaela Farm can provide to the public a level of expertise about and commitment to organic and biodynamic agriculture in their area which is not now available in the agricultural colleges, the Cooperative Extension Services, or the Departments of Agriculture at the federal or state levels. At Michaela, and sometimes elsewhere, one learns that these spiritually grounded models of ecological agriculture have already begun to play this role.

Vermicomposting bins (composting worms), rotational grazing workshops, strawbale housing construction, a very active CSA, nutritional workshops, spirituality programs consonant with creation spirituality, programs raising questions of justice in world food systems and industrial agriculture, nature trails, numerous classes on farming and ecology topics (rivaling the public agricultural extension service in their range and variety), a variety of the arts, and a deeply held sense of place permeates all.

Evolving mission statements over the past decade provide insight into the philosophical base of Michaela Farm. A 1991 statement reads: "We, the Sisters of St. Francis, entrusted with a family farm, and responding to a call from Mother Earth

> seek a new vision WITH (emphasis added) the land and those who wish to live in harmony with creation. We look to serve this land and ALL ITS IN-DIGENOUS SPECIES (emphasis added), both present and future generations, and all those seeking life-giving contact with nature. We do this by providing . . . educational opportunities for earth stewardship, . . . demonstrations of alternative growing methods, . . . demonstrations of other resources for healthy living, . . . space for secure and safe living of ALL SPECIES AND THEIR OFFSPRING (emphasis added), . . . opportunities for spirit-inspired development of the entire person, . . . food production in the spirit of the above. (Michaela Farm Advisory Group, April, 1992)

A 1995 mission statement refers to the farm as a place ". . . to join in promoting care for the land and all its inhabitants" and relates that "As we grow in awareness of our place on this land, we honor and sustain the patterns of nature."[12] And the Michaela Farm Mission Statement of 1999 opens with "Michaela Farm, a 300-acre organic farm, nurtures sustainable relationships among LAND, PLANTS, ANIMALS and HUMANS" (emphasis added).[13]

The ecological beauty of these philosophies may be found in the details of the farm plan, a plan which is oriented on spiritual, not economic grounds in order to accomplish the following:

1. To minimize outside inputs by utilizing farm resources in agricultural production through, for example, becoming self-sufficient for animal feed; assessing the feasibility of providing all farm community food needs (dairy, eggs, meat, grain, etc.); reducing use of chemical pest control materials while

implementing natural enemy control strategies; assessing the use of all energy inputs and the feasibility of alternative renewable energy sources; managing animal production for manure management and for compost production; managing green manure crops and hay crops in field rotations; fencing and watering pasture and implementing earthen dam reservoirs, with resultant irrigation systems to pastures and crops; managing for on-farm seed production; managing woodlands for firewood, lumber, understory herb production, wildlife habitat; and nature trails;

2. Managing farm resources to minimize soil erosion, enhance soil and water quality, and maintain wildlife habitat through a number of specific actions which constitute the very best of land and soil conservation techniques;

3. Operating the farm enterprises profitably for LONG-TERM (emphasis added) viability. This is basically vegetable production for direct marketing, and a grass-based cattle herd. It includes among other measures assessing the feasibility of a certified kitchen for processing daily and other foodstuffs; assessing the feasibility for acquiring/trading property for more arable acreage; and other economic measures.

There is further a detailed strategy on enhancing relationships, both with the broader human community and with the "other than human" world; a detailed strategy to move toward a balance between human needs and the needs of other life forms; a strategy to build community and promote personal development; a strategy to act in a just and socially responsible manner (including with respect to energy usage and in serious recycling).

There is also a detailed plan for spirituality, designed to nurture and live an earth-conscious spirituality. Such includes the fostering of a sense of sacred space; treating the land and all life forms with respect; providing times of mindfulness for all community members; celebrating the solstices and equinoxes; having an "Earth Chain" at all gatherings to insure an awareness of the presence of the entire community of life; developing ways to evoke the spirit of Saint Francis; celebrating the lives of animals on the farm; and, among other measures, evaluating the need for hermitages at Michaela Farm. There is, finally, within the plan a serious commitment to education and shared learning, including full programming to support it.

We see, therefore, at Michaela Farm, sound serious thought and talk, and a clearly determined and persistent willingness to "walk the talk," all contributing to placing Michaela Farm as an outstanding example of spiritually based ecological sustainability on the land, a model of sustainability par excellence.

As we reflect on these five serious examples of spiritually inspired models of sustainability described above, it is good to reflect on where they are located as well as on what they are doing. Most Americans have come to expect that ecological, environmental thinking, models, and advocacy come from New England, from the broader northeastern United States region, from California, or the Pacific Northwest coast of Oregon and Washington. They do not expect to receive this message from North Dakota, New Mexico, Kansas, Iowa, or Indiana. And yet, it is the heartland of America, north and south, the prairies, plains, deserts, and midwestern woodlands which, in this matter, is showing us the way. This is not to imply that nothing is happening elsewhere, but it is to imply that we can learn much from the heartland of our nation.

The community sustainability models of this chapter come from monastic, social justice, and "Sisters of Earth" models. Before moving on to a consideration of monasticism and ecology, and to a consideration of the relationship of social justice and eco-justice, it is now appropriate to explore more deeply the very widespread Sisters of Earth concept and the great wealth of communities which have sprung up across the nation in the wake of this new late twentieth century religious movement. But first we must turn to underlying theory. To some extent the thought of Thomas Berry and the practice emanating from it can be particularly helpful in this regard.

Chapter Four

THEORY BEHIND
THE PRACTICE

A central and, in some ways implicit if not explicit, guiding philosophy for the Sisters of Earth network and similar communities emanates from the work and thought of "geologian" (i.e., theologian of the earth) Thomas Berry. Author of the seminal works *The Dream of the Earth*, *Befriending the Earth* (with Thomas Clark), *The Universe Story* (with Brian Swimme), and *The Great Work*, Berry is a cultural historian and student of East Asian culture and religion who has become, in recent decades, an important environmental philosopher and ethicist. Berry the scholar is increasingly widely known. Less known is the fact that Berry is a monk, although he has not lived in a monastic community for many decades. His work constitutes a body of thought which provides an entreé into the linkage of sustainability and spirituality. To understand the Sisters of Earth network and the movement they represent, and likeminded efforts, it can be helpful, therefore, to understand in a general way the ideas, the thought of Thomas Berry, for the practical work and the communities of the Sisters of Earth are in part and often inadvertently the application of Thomas Berry's principles to the world. Berry provides theory and a rationale. The women of Sisters of Earth and their associates provide the practice, which, coincidentally or otherwise, puts Berry's thought into practice. (This is not to say the sisters are not, as well, significantly influenced by their own orders' charisms, and by the thinking of others, including Wendell Berry, Terry Tempest Williams, Fritjof Capra, E. F. Schumacher, Edward Abbey, and, historically, Hildegard of Bingen, Julian of Norwich, Saint Clare, and others.)

Berry models from Thomas Aquinas, the great Christian theologian who held that the order of the universe is the ultimate and noblest perfection in things and that the whole universe together participates in and manifests the divine more than any one single being. At one and the same time, this is a Christian theological underpinning for the preservation of biodiversity and conservation biology and, as well, an ultimate rationale for creation spirituality. And again from Thomas Aquinas, Berry sees the universe as the purpose of Creation and the object of redemption.

Berry's understanding of the universe is described in three basic principles:

1. *differentiation*—the universe is not homogeneous but is rather composed of clearly articulated entities, each of which is unique and irreplaceable;

2. *subjectivity*—each of the component members of the universe has its own interiority, its spontaneity, its subjectivity;

3. *communion*—each member of the universe community is bonded inseparably with every other member of the community, the entire universe is genetically related, each member is cousin to every other being, and each member is immediately present to and influencing every other being in the universe, without, we are told by modern physics, crossing intervening space.

One's outer and inner world are reciprocal in their functioning and in their destiny. All is in all. Everything is implicated in everything else, everything is a microcosm of everything else, as the physicist David Bohm would say. As above, so below; as within, so without. All things move in sympathetic relation to each other. Individuals incorporate the whole universe in some sense and must exhibit the order of the cosmos in their lives. This interconnectedness is so strong that the human community is unintelligible without the entire earth community, leading one to believe that the proper role of human intelligence is to enhance the natural world rather than to exploit it.

Berry holds to an analogous view on world religions, namely, that each of the world religions is differentiated unique and irreplaceable in its expression and has its own inner life or subjectivity. However, its full self depends for its completion on its bonding, its communion, with the other traditions. He defines "communion" as organic connectedness and not social contract.

With respect to the theological constructs of immanence and transcendence, both of which are integral to Christianity, Berry writes that when transcendence (i.e., God above and beyond, there before and for all eternity) is overemphasized, as has been the case for several hundreds of years, God becomes irrelevant and remote. This is the "sky'God" image of Christian theologian Sallie McFague. When immanence (the Creator in the created, God in all) is overemphasized, then the symbols, images, and rituals become mere idols and myths and the Divine is identified with and thus reduced to the things of the universe itself. Berry dwells significantly, however, on the importance of immanence, asserting that the doctrine of God's immanence maintains that God is not distant from creation but that all creation participates somehow in the divine reality. This is balanced by God's transcendence which allows creation to operate according to the intrinsic nature of its own being. But, to come full circle, what we know to be true about the universe reveals something about the nature of God. According to Berry: "Why do we have such a wonderful idea of God? Because we live in such a gorgeous world. We wonder at the magnificence of whatever it is that brought the world into being. This leads to a sense of adoration. We have a sense of immense gratitude that we participate in such a beautiful world. This adoration, this gratitude, we call religion."[1]

Berry contends that we need a religious and an imaginative sensitivity to other creatures, a "feeling for the organism," as he calls it. Part of this feeling must come from a bioregional sense, an attachment to and a dependency on one's own place, one's own region. From such a bioregional sense, Berry contends that all human professions, institutions, and activities must be integral with the Earth as primary self-nourishing, self-governing and self-fulfilling community, and that "all the professions must be realigned to reflect the primacy of the Earth."[2]

Those familiar with the principal and better known works of Thomas Berry are not accustomed to the direct and overt religious references (God-talk) present in the foregoing. Berry seeks to avoid the divisiveness and exclusivity, the separation that such talk can inspire and thus avoids this kind of talk in his secular work. Indeed, Tom often tells the story of being approached by a member of one of his audiences who appeared confused after his speech. Berry had been speaking very inclusively of all faith and belief systems and his listener, puzzled and confused, asked him. "What DO you believe?" Tom smiled wistfully and perhaps a little mischievously and responded, "Madam, I believe in everything! Tell me something and I'll believe it."[3] Most people would be put off by such a response but a deeper understanding of Berry reveals how true and, at the same time, how meaningful it is and can be, but only at a deeper level. Berry, like the Benedictine monk and philosopher Bede Griffiths, does not see the contradiction in the statement which most of us immediately sense. Deeper probing is invited.

It is important to point out in the context of this book that women religious are often at home with and are fully understanding of this language, of Berry's "God-talk" in the foregoing, and so it is both the secular and the religious philosopher Thomas Berry who speaks to them. It is appropriate, therefore, that this capability to relate through religion is not unimportant in the context of earth-based religious communities, including the Sisters of Earth network. (This is not to exclude the use of Thomas Berry's thought by many mainline Protestant denominations, by secular groups, and by others across the United States.)

Sisters of Earth who are members of religious orders draw their theory and their inspiration, of course, from the Bible, from Holy Scripture. As Roman Catholic, culturally and theologically, they are also inspired by the lives of the saints and from Catholic social teaching. Members of religious orders draw also from the charisms of their foundresses, their heritage, and their communities down through the ages. But with respect to the Creation, they draw insight and inspiration from cultural historian and philosopher Thomas Berry, as do the lay women among them who are equally interested in and sympathetic to these influences. This insight and inspiration is supplemented by others, by Dominican Sister Miriam Therese MacGillis, by Trappist monk Thomas Merton, by Jesuit Teilhard de Chardin, by Dorothy Day, by Protestant theologian Dietrich Bonhoeffer, by Jewish philosophers Martin Buber and Abraham Heschel, and by numerous important eco-spiritual philosophers of today. But among the more basic to their formation as Sisters of Earth is Thomas Berry, implicitly if not always explicitly. And thus to understand them it is important to gain a basic understanding of the work and thought of Thomas Berry.

Although Thomas Berry's work appears in many articles, papers, audio and videotapes that are in wide distribution, the core of his work, his ideas, his philosophies is accessible in three books: *The Dream of the Earth*

(1988); *The Universe Story* (coauthored with scientist Brian Swimme, 1992); and *The Great Work* (1999). From these three works one can access all of his central ideas and in a form understandable in the secular world.

Thomas Berry is a cultural historian with a long career of scholarship in East Asian philosophy and religion. He served on the faculties of three universities in the New York area (Fordham, St. John's, and Seton Hall). Since the normal age of retirement, Berry has consummated a new career, evolved from the first career and now almost a quarter century in duration, in the area of ecological thought and its practical application, sustainability. His involvement as cofounder of Green Mountain Monastery in Vermont may be a culminating development in his career and a return to his monastic roots. Berry has become a philosopher of science and of ecological ethics, and is commanding respect in this area. Although wary of our use of technology, he is a strong celebrant of science and of the awe and enchantment which he finds true science must inspire. He also sees his work as highly integral with the cutting edge of modern science, especially ecological thought, quantum physics/quantum mechanics, and mathematical theory, and his collaboration with physicist and mathematical cosmologist Brian Swimme, which led to their joint book, *The Universe Story: From the Primordial Flaring Forth to the Ecozoic Era—A Celebration of the Unfolding of the Cosmos*, is testament to this integration. (In fact, *The Universe Story* achieves such a high level of integration that it is difficult to determine which author, the historian or the physicist, wrote what.)

Thomas Berry has written that, in the phenomenal order, the universe is the only text without a context. It is the only self-referent being in the phenomenal order. This is, of course, the only conclusion one could reach from a careful consideration of the meaning and principles of ecology, but it is rarely expressed in this powerful way. One might also note the conditionary phrase "in the phenomenal order" which means the complete statement does not deny the possibility of a creator God, for such a God, certainly in the Judaeo-Christian heritage, is clearly outside the phenomenal order and not subject to the understanding or comprehension of mere mortals. The phrase also refers to the universe as a "text," a book of instruction, a guide, a teacher, one of the basic principles of ecology. And he writes of that all-encompassing context as encompassing mystery, as the sacred, as the divine.

Humans are placed in Berry's work as that being in whom the universe reflects upon and celebrates itself. This is a reference, of course, to the unique (as far as we know) ability of humans to think, to reason, to consider the past, to consider the future. And it reflects a belief that the universe, in its celebratory ability, is alive and uses humans, a part of itself, to carry out this role. Berry also places the human as derivative, seeing the universe, the bigger whole, as primary.

As a cultural historian, Berry tells us that all earlier peoples experienced the universe as the cosmological order, as the basic context of the divine. As such, the universe (that is, Nature) is revelatory along with Scripture. Thus, the universe, or Nature, reveals the Divine, reveals God, to us. Looking at the human, Berry sees our imagination, our poetry, our music, our creativity, as all reflective of the Earth, of Nature, because we are so connected to the Earth. Through this connection, we have a covenantal relationship with the Divine, and if we are to be resurrected (a central teaching of Christianity), then the universe, Nature, has to be resurrected for we are nothing without or outside the universe. Nothing has meaning without relationship to everything else.

Seeing the universe as not mechanistic but spiritual, as not merely physical or material, Berry sees the adoption of this sense of the universe as sacred as being the most important work of our time. He believes that to do anything effective at the present time requires something profoundly of a religious nature and thus that we need new religious sensitivities toward Nature in all religions.

Berry believes that nothing can ever be separated from anything else, that you can feel isolated but that you can never be isolated. That is why the bonding of things is so powerful; it is the primary law of being. More important than basic Christian communities, therefore, are basic life communities.

Berry holds that we suffer from an addictive pathology: we know what we're doing to the soil, the planet, the ecosystem, but we go on doing it anyway. Our glory has become the desolation of the Earth, Berry writes, and we and our institutions, our professions, our programs, our activities must now be judged primarily by the extent to which they inhibit, ignore, or foster a mutually enhancing human-earth relationship. The less beautiful the planet becomes, the less chance the realization of the Divine will be possible.

Berry sees our cultural genetic coding as failing us, leading to a need to re-invent ourselves to carry out the task at hand. This need becomes doubly important given that the universities and the churches are so implicated in the processes of destruction that they cannot help us out of the quagmire; they must be reformed themselves.

The only way to live is with the ever-renewing processes of Nature, in an integral life. It is intimacy which is important, not stewardship or veneration. The universe is a subject, not an object—if we don't accept that, we're doomed. We must, therefore, reconnect our sympathetic rapport with the natural world and recognize that the world has a spontaneity; it has a soul. Diversity is precious and sacred; the primordial sacred community is the universe, as opposed to the human alone; our first obligation is to have reverence for everything; and the path to the Creator is through the created. To preserve the natural world as the primary revelation of the Divine must be the basic concern of religion.

Berry is an outspoken believer in science which he sees as offering a new revelation of the Divine. He praises the microscope for taking us deep into the interior, and the telescope (and especially the Hubble) for taking us outward to galactic systems. In linking science and religion, he makes clear his belief that one doesn't get to Heaven except through Earth, a belief, to use his terminology, that would be the hallmark of any decent religion. With modern science for the first time we're experiencing the total story of the universe through our capacity to communicate with it and to understand our capacity to listen to it. We now begin listening, looking, thinking about the universe processes as the universe reveals the deep mysteries of existence, and as we come to find that the universe story is our own personal story.

Thomas Berry is wedded to the idea of story, the primary mode of human understanding. We must understand the poetry of the universe; we must understand this story, our sacred story, for that is the new understanding of the universe. What the mountains say is important, what the trees say is important. The Earth is primarily a magical, mystical reality.

Berry believes it's important that we deal with the current ecological challenge out of the religious traditions, but that there's a twofold process that must take place: it can't be read exclusively from the traditions—one must read the traditions in the context of the story, and the verbal traditions cannot be primary. All religions have something to teach us. There is a complementarity between Hinduism, Buddhism, and the Judaeo-Christian heritage. He connects the outer and the inner world as parts of the same thing: if in our outer world we cannot see the stars because of pollution, then we cannot be inspired by them in our inner world; ditto the song of birds, the butterflies, and so forth. By communing or communicating with Nature, we can also communicate with God.

In this tight linkage of science and religion, Thomas Berry gives us three basic governing moral principles:

1. Everything carries its own uniqueness and individuality, and each reality is distinct (that is, differentiated).

2. Everything carries the whole numinous divine dimension of the universe within itself.

3. Everything is bonded to everything else.

In his recent book, *The Great Work*, Berry identifies today's great task at hand to carry out the transition from a period of human devastation of the Earth to a period when humans would be present to the planet in a mutually beneficial manner. Reiterating that what happens to the nonhuman happens to the human, that what happens to the outer world happens to the inner world, he sees our task as becoming integral with the larger earth community. Other than human models of being are seen as having no rights. Berry grants that we have rights but that all rights are limited and relative, and that we have no right to disturb the basic functioning of the biosystem. We cannot own the Earth or any part of it in any absolute manner.

While we expect our place to give itself to us, we have no sense of giving ourselves to our place. Therefore, some sense of the planet Earth as the intimate place of our dwelling needs to be fostered. In this process, the well-being of the soil and the plants growing on Earth must be a primary concern for humans who must come to recognize that to disrupt this process is not only to break the Covenant of the Earth, but also to imperil life, for the human and other components of Earth form a single community of life which is central to all.

In this recent work, Berry again cites Aquinas that "the order of the universe is the ultimate and noblest perfection in things" and that "the whole universe together participates in the divine goodness and represents it better than any single being whatsoever."[4]

In an ode to concrete practicality, Berry writes of the primacy of the following.

*   organic farming

*   community supported agriculture

*   solar/hydrogen energy systems

- re-design of our cities
- elimination of the automobile in its present form
- restoration of local village economies
- education for a post-petroleum way of life, a way of life which, unlike our own, would not be fundamentally based on the use of oil
- a jurisprudence that recognizes the rights of natural modes of being

All these aspects are a necessity and, as well, a characteristic of earth-based religious communities. (In essence, this is not far from the afore-mentioned Wendell Berry's principles of community sustainability.)

Perhaps the foremost interpreter of Thomas Berry to these earth-based religious communities across the nation is the Dominican Sister Miriam Therese MacGillis, founder of Genesis Farm in New Jersey. She is the inspiration for numerous Dominican and other women's religious order-established communities coast-to-coast that form the loose network called Sisters of Earth (see next chapter). Important and directly pertinent philosophies of Sr. Miriam Therese which carry application of Thomas Berry to these communities include:

- the inherent spirituality of the universe, which we know analytically does not need to rely on faith
- our need for Nature as a vehicle to worship God
- the role of the natural world as an assist to the capacity of the human to image and to become like God
- the necessity of the human to return to her bioregion, her home
- the centrality of a sense of community, for it's only in having each other that people survive
- the capacity to see the interiority of the other as revelatory, a type of purity of heart, for when you see God you do not abuse
- the entrapment of accumulation
- the importance of the influence of Teilhard de Chardin whom Tom Berry believes represents the greatest change in Christian theology since Paul

- the importance of but at the same time the inadequacy of the world of ideas

- the importance of but at the same time the inadequacy of our religious traditions

- the realization that it takes three years to learn the basic principles of biodynamic agriculture and ten years to apply those principles to a specific site

- the awareness that agriculture is a priestly activity, that the healing of the soil, the creation of gardens, becomes a role, a priestly one

- the importance of attunement in order to bring oneself into obedience to the cycles, the seasons, to weather, nature, and so forth

- the understanding that if the Earth is malnourished or devitalized, how can the food we grow carry the spirit dimension into us

- the necessary centrality of grains and vegetables to our diet rather than meat[5]

There are many more that can be added but the above provides a picture.

From the earliest years of Christianity (perhaps the second century A.D.) we have been confronted with Tertullian's question: Does the sacred have something to say to the secular? And the further question: if the answer be yes, then who might do the asking? The next chapter, an examination of the Sisters of Earth, their network, and their work, provides a possible answer, and many more community models.

Chapter Five

WE WILL NOT SAVE
WHAT WE DO NOT LOVE:
SISTERS OF EARTH IN
OUR LAND

Sisters of Earth are lovers par excellence, and modelers of the art of sustainability for others.

According to Sr. Toni Nash, a cofounder of the Sisters of Earth network, "The Sisters of Earth is an informal network of women who share a deep concern for the ecological and spiritual crisis of our times and who wish to support one another in work toward healing the human spirit and restoring the Earth's life-support systems. We are teachers, gardeners, artists, writers, administrators, workshop givers, monastics, activists, mothers. . . . in the United States, Canada, and beyond. This network of sharing and support is open to all women whose life and work would identify them as sisters of Earth. We hold a general meeting every two years in different parts of the country to help local chapters and support systems to become established. We encourage local groups to meet during the off years."[1]

Of central importance to any study of the Sisters of Earth network is that they represent one of the purest examples of life lived according to ecological principle, to sustainability principle, of any community of people in our nation and culture. They also represent among the purest forms of practice of life lived according to the teachings of Francis of Assisi, Teilhard de Chardin, Wendell Berry, Helen and Scott Nearing, and

Thomas Berry. But, if one wanted to sum up the sisters' philosophy, one might do so from a saying of early Christianity:

"We do not want words alone for there are too many words among people today. What we need is action, for that is what we are looking for, not words which do not bear fruit."[2]

As one approaches Sisters of Earth and their communities and practices, it is wise to use underlying parameters of indicators in order to assess them and their work. The indicators chosen are purely secular indicators and represent both an individual and a communal approach.

In evaluating these communities, indicators of sustainability one might apply are the aforementioned of Helen and Scott Nearing as summarized in their compilation *Guiding Principles for a Good Life,* and the seventeen principles of sustainability or set of rules promulgated by Wendell Berry in his essay "Conserving Communities." As we have seen in a preceding chapter, the Nearing principles pertain more to how we should live on a personal basis. The Wendell Berry principles are better organized at the community rather than the individual level and can provide a measure of how the Sisters of Earth network of individuals and communities, monastic communities, social justice, and secular communities function within the broader community as well as within themselves.

Supplementing these two sets of indicators are additional reliance on certain elements of the Eightfold Noble Path to Right Livelihood (Buddhist), the principle of subsidiarity (Christian), and the Sermon on the Mount (Christian), all of which are held in high regard implicitly if not always explicitly by the members of these communities.

A number of years ago Thomas Berry recognized the important role of women religious and their communities in the transition to the Ecozoic era with the publication of his essay "Women Religious: Their Future Role."[3] This document has helped inspire Dominican, Franciscan, Sisters of St. Joseph, Benedictine women and, as well, Sisters of Charity, Sisters of Notre Dame, Sisters of Mercy, Sisters of Loretto, Sisters of Providence, and members of many other orders to chart a path of ecological community building which has led to the present existence of Sisters of Earth individuals and communities on the land and across the nation, communities that "green" wherever they are. Several hundred Catholic nuns and a smaller number of lay women have joined to embrace the Earth as their ministry since their original founding in 1994 by Carondelet St. Joseph Sisters Mary Southard, Mary Lou Dolan, and Toni Nash.

Over the past two centuries, an enormous amount of work in education, in healing, in social work, and in spiritual guidance has been carried out worldwide by religious congregations of women. These religious communities, along with everyone else, are called upon to accept a new role, that of stopping the devastation that humans are inflicting on the planet. Women religious are hearing the call that humans be present to the Earth in a mutually enhancing manner. Tom Berry has often referred to the universe as a single multiform celebratory event: "Our role is to enter into this celebration in a special mode of conscious self-awareness, for this celebration is the divine liturgy, the purpose of all existence, celebration begun in time but continued through eternity."[4] In doing this Berry harkens to what he calls a "uniquely Christian process": the work of Christian religious communities in the centuries after the decline of the Roman Empire to become the principal forces in creating an entire civilization, the medieval world. This can be done only by moving our basic life orientation from a dominant anthropocentrism to a dominant ecocentrism, achievable only by listening to the voices of the universe, the voices of the Earth, and all its multitude of living and nonliving modes of expression. He says that we should be listening to the stars in the heavens, the sun, and the moon, to the mountains and the plains, the forests, rivers, and seas that surround us wherever we are, to the meadows and the flowering grasses, the songbirds, the lion, and the tiger, to the insects, and by their music especially in the evening and the early hours of the night.

The primary past role of women religious has been in educating, healing, and guiding spiritually and physically in the human community, whereas their primary role in the immediate present might well be to preserve the Earth from further devastation. This has become a condition for fulfilling any other role, for there cannot be Christians unless there are humans, no faith without intelligence; nor can there be humans without the integral functioning of the living world about us. Thus, the natural and human imperatives are prior to and a necessary condition for any Christian imperative. Thomas Berry writes: "We cannot now be integral Christians because we are not integral humans. We are not integral humans because we have alienated ourselves from the larger life community."[5] If the life systems are not saved, then everything else is irrelevant, and thus "If a women's religious congregation committed to the saving of the natural world was unthinkable in former centuries, it is now unthinkable that any women's congregation should not be committed as a primary concern and purpose to the saving of the natural world."[6]

Human-earth relations have a claim on our attention prior to divine-human or interhuman relations simply because our experience of the universe supercedes in time our experience of ourselves or of the Divine. Saint Paul asserts in his Epistle to the Romans that from the things that are made we come to know the Maker.

Berry identifies a special role for women in these matters, as the eco-feminist movement joins two of the most powerful movements of our times "in effecting the transition from a nonviable to a viable mode of existence for the planetary community." This is Berry's transition from the terminal Cenozoic to the emerging Ecozoic era in earth history.

Berry suggests that women may be more attuned to the voices of the Earth in a way that is especially needed at this time. With this gift, the "single greatest service that women religious could make to the larger destinies of the human, the Christian, and the earth community would be the recovery of our human and Christian intimacy with the spontaneities of all those wonderful participants in the universe of being."[7] A unity of the human with its environment will, for the forseeable future, "be the context of all the various activities of women's religious communities."[8] Numbers of Sisters of various religious orders responded to this call.[9]

It should be mentioned here that there is a small corollary male effort, much less well known, called "Brothers of Earth," involving both religious and lay. Founded by Jim Conlon and Jesuit John Surette, S. J. and based at the Sophia Center of Holy Names College in Oakland, California, Brothers of Earth are also directly inspired by Thomas Berry. According to Director Conlon, "Brothers of Earth" is a developing "non-organization" of men who are engaged in ecological spirituality and who gather annually for information, support, and the possibility of common action. They represent a broad spectrum of careers and commitments. Among the religious orders represented among them are the Passionists, the same order to which Thomas Berry belongs. They differ, however, from their female counterparts in one basic way, they are significantly less involved in physical communities on the land, and thus do not offer models of sustainability of pertinence to this volume. It is conceivable, however, they may sufficiently influence landed communities of men religious who may experience the conversion so much more prevalent among women's religious communities.

Thomas Berry is enamored of story, of the universe story, of the story the universe tells of itself. To Christians and to women religious, it is also the story of the Trinity in its three most basic tendencies: differentiation, interiority, and universal bonding, a manifest of the ultimate divine forces that brought the world into being, more commonly expressed by these Christian women as Father, Son, and Holy Spirit. And it is, as well, the Christ story, in accord with the Fathers of the Church and Christian theologians everywhere. Dante in his *Divine Comedy* "tells us that in his vision of the divine reality he saw therein 'all the scattered leaves of the universe bound by love in one volume.' Such is the origin and end of all our human or Christian or religious communities."[10]

There is little wonder that Catholic women religious are answering the call. Sparked by Sr. Miriam Therese MacGillis, Dominican nun from New Jersey, the first Sisters of Earth type of community became established as Genesis Farm at Blairstown in northern New Jersey in the early 1990s. Genesis Farm soon became an inspiration for these Christian earth-based communities, just as Sr. Miriam Therese and, indeed, the Dominican Order, became an inspiration for other Dominicans and women of numerous other religious orders to follow and do likewise. From a long line of Dominican communities spread from Massachusetts and New Jersey west to Kansas and involving many of the states in between, the movement spread, developing special strength in the midwestern region from western Pennsylvania to Iowa and Minnesota. Increasingly, there are such communities in the Northeast and on the western Great Plains, the Far West and, to a smaller degree, in the Southwest. There remain few such communities in the Southeast, perhaps coincident with the scarcity of Catholic religious communities in that region.

The Sisters of Earth in their formative years asked of themselves, their peers, and their orders: How can we see the "cry of the earth" and the "cry of the people" not as two separate cries, sometimes pitted against each other, but as two faces of the same living planet we call home, struggling to survive? Is it enough to make an option for the poor—a traditional Christian and Catholic directive—unless we also make an option for preserving the Earth that sustains the poor and all other creatures? How does concern for the entire earth community relate to our charism, the raison d'être, the rationale, for the existence of our order and our community?

Sisters of Earth was born as an organization (if it can be called that—a loose non-hierarchical network is more descriptive) at a meeting of sixty mainly women religious from seventeen states and Canada which took place at St. Gabriel's Center for Ecology and Contemplation (part of St. Gabriel's Monastery, a monastic community of the Passionist Order) at Clark's Summit, Pennsylvania, July 13–16, 1994.[11] The mutual commitment of these women was to "reverence all land with which we are in relationship and all the life it supports." This was the first effort to gather already independently operating communities and centers into a single organic network. These women came from diverse backgrounds in the performance of ecological work: of experiences on the land, of efforts to educate young children, of work with inner-city gardens for the poor, of community-supported and congregation-supported agriculture projects, of solar habitat construction, of establishing earth literacy programs at university level, of outreach to local parishes, of work with nongovernmental environmental organizations, at the United Nations, and of numerous types and kinds of artistic endeavors. In the presence of one another, it is told, they drew on their own resources, as storytellers, as liturgists, as musicians, as dancers, to ritualize important moments of each day and to celebrate the beauty of the place. A common conviction among these women was their belief that as women pool their energies and resources in a common effort, as they join together as Sisters of Earth, hidden power will be released to bring about a changed relationship between humans and the rest of creation.

Since that event, several more meetings have been held in other parts of the country, generally on a biennial basis. The year 2000 meeting, the Fourth International Conference of the Sisters of Earth, was held at La Casa de Maria Center in Santa Barbara, California, and revealed:

> A new spirituality is emerging among us. We are not just making a place for Earth concerns among our familiar prayers. In many cases, we are laying a completely new foundation, building new spiritual practices, and developing new sensitivities to the voice of God speaking in creation. It is a spirituality born of wonder at the face of the Divine being revealed in our time and of grief at the destruction of this beauty. . . . (O)ur members . . . through their own evolving spiritual practices, are helping to lay a foundation for a new relationship with ourselves, the Holy and the Earth.[12]

Sr. Miriam Therese MacGillis' Genesis Farm in New Jersey did in fact become somewhat of a genesis of the movement in practice, establishing it as a land-based movement which invariably includes the growing of food at its core. Genesis Farm, as well a center for the study of eco-literacy, and its peers elsewhere implicitly put Thomas Berry's philo-sophical theory into practice, on the land, in the ecosystem and in the community of real people. Dominican women's communities naturally formed an early core, remaining today an important centerpiece. They have been joined by many other women's religious communities. Each of these communities is place-based and highly values and advocates a strong sense of place, in addition to representing different orders or charisms of religious heritage, so each community differs somewhat from the others. However, a reasonably clear image of these communities may be formed from a study of the characteristics they hold in common in both theory and in practice.

The three decades old environmental movement in the United States and the decade long green, deep ecology, and sustainability movements in this country have both generated a great quantity of talk, one might be tempted to say all talk and little action. Discussions, debates, books, ar-ticles, films, audio and video tapes, and so forth,—talk, talk, talk. The three times older environmental movement, it is true, featured action in the form of the expenditure of great amounts of public and private funds for public works, sewage treatment plants, air pollution control, land and habitat acquisition, catalytic converters on automobiles, and in other ex-penditures. If the expenditure of funds be action, then this is action. But in all of this expenditure there emerged no environmental ethic, no change of values, no change in lifestyle or behavior. In fact, this great ex-penditure likely provided an excuse not to take real action, not to change from established ingrained behavioral patterns.

Those who "walk their talk," who practice what they preach, espe-cially in the environmental-ecological area, have been exceedingly rare. And for good reason. For walking the talk, ecologically speaking, re-quires an ability to resist the direction of mainstream society, and takes a good deal of personal energy, patience, and persistence. Few individuals and even fewer groups have what it takes. A notable exception is women's religious communities, communities of American women who have been heroically and courageously walking their talk in many other difficult areas of life and facing and overcoming exceedingly difficult challenges. Some number of these women, individually and collectively, have moved heart and soul into ecological concern. This concern takes the form of living and modeling an ecologically positive and sustainable lifestyle, in sharp contradistinction to the way we expect most people to live in our society. The women to whom I refer are Christian and are members of Catholic women's religious communities. They are celibate and have made a life-time commitment (whether through vows or not) to the requirements of and charism of their respective orders. They are, for the most part, not cloistered, and are very much in the society we know and are active participants in that society. Some are monastic. They are spread out in their communities across much of the United States, although the midwestern states have the most.

People with an outwardly religious appearance in terms of their behavior are sometimes thought of as "people of faith." Those of no such religious appearance may be thought of as lacking in faith. And yet all people are people of faith. It is part of human nature, part of the very definition of being human, to have faith, to be people of faith. The only question is, What do we place our faith in, and is it good? Is our faith grounded in something bigger than we are, normally thought of as religious or spiritual faith? Or is it reduced, is it placed in something smaller and more quantifiably measurable like technology, or a narrow view of science, the economy, growth, shopping, money, or on a false notion of efficiency? Surely we put our faith belief somewhere and act out this belief everyday, in what comes to be seen as our values.

We have seen that there are a growing number of religious communities across the United States. These are communities, particularly of women, who are professed members of Christian (basically Catholic) communities who are becoming seriously and deeply committed to living lightly, to living sustainably, to living within the principles of ecology. Such is not an easy task and requires great commitment, effort, hard work, and perseverance. These communities are exceedingly ecumenical in their nature, often interfaith in practice, across Christianity, across numerous non-Christian faith beliefs, and very accepting of those who are skeptical and/or less sure of all religious denominations, categories, or designations. Although Catholic at their core, with both an upper case and lower case "c," these communities often have significant interest in Eastern philosophies and/or indigenous peoples' spirituality. Their sometime interest in Zen is not unlike a similar interest which has developed since the time of Thomas Merton in both men's and women's monastic communities. These communities are strong believers in creation spirituality, that is, that the way to Christ, the way to God, is through God's creation, and, like good ecologists, they regard Nature as teacher, as guide, alongside scripture and tradition. They also take literally the call to stand in awe of God's creation, to consider it sacred, to reverence it as God's, not as ours. They put great emphasis on the theological precept of immanence, that is, the Creator in the created, God in all. They do not reject the companion theological precept of transcendence but believe in the need to return the balance between these two nonexclusionary and companion precepts in contrast to society's centuries old emphasis on transcendence over immanence. Likewise, they know the insufficiency of creation-oriented spirituality alone and believe and act in support of both redemption-oriented and resurrection-centered spirituality, as will be discussed later.

Without doubt some of the strongest and most persistent examples or models of sustainability in the United States are to be found in the series of Dominican, Franciscan, and Benedictine women's communities in the United States which have deliberately set out on a path to ecological sustainability, interpreting such as God's command to them, indeed to all of us. These women-led and women-inspired ecumenical communities are committed to sustainable, organic food production, both for themselves and others, through their increasing commitment to community-supported agriculture. They are committed to permaculture (i.e., permanent ecological agriculture); often to the Rudolf Steiner systems of biodynamic agriculture; often to fully organic certification for their production; to encouraging, developing, and practicing subscriber, or community-supported agriculture (CSAs); to the maximization of diversity in their deliberately small-scale operations; and to total composting of their food waste and other organics back into their soil.[13]

Likewise, they are strongly committed to ecological habitat design; to ecologically acceptable construction patterns (including straw-bale construction); to major energy conservation techniques; and to complete or near complete reliance on renewable rather than nonrenewable sources of energy (i.e., active and passive solar, biomass, wood, wind, etc., rather than fossil fuel or nuclear energy). Members of these communities, both religious and lay, women and men (there are male members) are additionally engaged, in building construction and maintenance, land management, and in a variety of other activities, including many forms of education and teaching. Of course, as might be expected, members are engaged in prayer. How might they pray? All of these communities have their own schedules for community prayer and an expectation of time to be set aside for individual prayer. They do pray also in the performance of all of their sustainability activities. I do not refer only to the recitation of prayerful words, or to chant, but to the act itself, of gardening, of cooking, of environmental/ecological nurturance, as prayer. For they, like countless monastic communities of men and women through the ages, regard prayer as action as much as, or even more than words or chant. This is not to suggest that time is not devoted to more conventional prayer and chant but to emphasize the central importance of offering action as prayer, a notion always present in Christianity but often de-emphasized. And, of course, action as prayer makes possible the labor necessary to live ecologically. Like the Amish, the members of these communities regard labor as a benefit, not as a cost, labor being a gift from God to all who can perform it, for its own healthful values to the laborer and for the good of the community. (This is in synchrony with those monastic communities which are ecologically based and thus labor intensive, but clearly not synchronous with those monastic communities which spend so many hours in chapel in conventional prayer that they often do not have sufficient remaining time to do the work necessary to maintain the land, the crops, and so forth, as ecology would require.)

These communities are not simply intentional communities for those wishing to flee from the world; most perform social ministries which put them foursquare in the real world. Central to these social ministries is the concept that human healing (mental, physical, spiritual) can occur through healing the Earth. One can well encounter visitors to and occupants of these communities who have been through or are experiencing traumatic circumstances. These might include people abandoned for one reason or another, marginalized people of all kinds, recovering addicts, former prisoners, and even current prisoners, people who can provide needed labor but who themselves are moved along on the path of healing through provision of this labor. Prisoners might range from juvenile offenders performing court-mandated public service in the community without police or court supervision (other than periodic reporting), to medium security incarcerated prisoners accompanied by armed prison guards. (It is said that incarcerated prisoners vie for this opportunity and can get it through good behavior.) But far more common in the healing ministry of these ecological communities are abandoned and/or battered women who, to some degree, have a natural attraction to the communities due to their inherent nature as women-directed and women-inspired institutions, and as safe welcoming places.

Direction in the conventional sense in these communities is nonexistent, for they are exceptionally non-hierarchical in theory and practice. They reject linearity as well as hierarchy and conduct themselves in a consensus mode of self-governance, under the ultimate supervision of a larger order elsewhere. But this "ultimate supervision" more often than not tends to be loose, informal, and distant. This is a testament to the women who have committed themselves to these communities, such is the high regard and esteem in which they are held. They very often operate with a high degree of autonomy.

What is the nature of these women? They vary widely in age. They are committed members of their orders and are celibate. They are religious in every sense but this should not signal to the reader a tight holding onto a narrow doctrine, nor to any rigidity, for their religion is in the true sense of "*religio*," a binding together with their roots, with their Creator, and the sense of awe and humility that that binding brings about. They are fully Christian but do not hold to hierarchy or institutions with any vigor, recognizing the problems and failings (and often antiecological nature) of both. Often, if older, they have had significant experience with overseas missions, with indigenous cultures and their spiritualities, sometimes with the Eastern cultures and spiritualities, and have no lack of understanding of or experience with the very poor, the oppressed, the marginalized of all kinds. Needless to say, they are strong, and they are courageous. What perhaps marks them differently from others is their deepening realization of connectedness with the entirety of creation, with the cosmos, with ecology writ large. They bring to sustainability, to sustainable living, to ecology, and to ecological thought a combination of faith and courage. This combination has dynamic force, the force of dynamite, insuring not only the strength of the models of sustainability they have to offer, but also a strong model of resistance to the status quo, to the conventional wisdom. They are a threat to the powerful forces of unsustainability with which we live everyday. The difference between these women and most of the rest of us is their dynamic mixture of faith and courage. Such a mixture is unstoppable and, being as well equipped through experience as they are, these people and their communities stand before us as potentially among the strongest examples, demonstrations, and models of how to live sustainably that we will be able to find.

Such earth-oriented religious communities may best be defined by what they have in common with one another, for what they have in common is considerable and significant and reflects both theory and practice. Such communities have an enormous quantity of practice and practices in common, and, as well, a significant amount of common theory.

THEORY IN COMMON

Theoretical commonalities would include:

1. Linkages to justice and the connection between social justice and eco-justice. Justice for farmers, justice for farm workers, justice for the recipients of food, justice for creation—all are truly pervasive, and provide a basic foundation for the establishment and operation of such communities. Justice for humans is part of the universal teaching of their religious faith while eco-justice is a newer late twentieth century form of justice, although with roots much earlier.

2. Linkages to Christianity not only to the charism, cultural history, and practice of the individual order but also to the order's founder, abstracted, and interpreted to support the ecological and eco-justice approach of the work at hand.

3. Linkages to ecumenism, to ecumenical approaches, not only to and through all Christian denominations, but to and through interfaith linkages as well. This includes Eastern philosophies, an interest in which is often present and is occasionally strong, including the practice of Zen and indigenous peoples' spirituality. This sometimes arises through considerable grassroots experience of the founding and participating religious, and arises as well from an openness of spirit which is so welcoming that it is common for the majority of people being served by these projects, joining them, and supporting them, and interning in them to be non-Catholic. The latter is positive proof of the high level of ecumenism found in these projects and in these communities.

4. Adherence to the basic principles of ecology, as expressed by Barry Commoner and many other scientists and philosophers, is universal and is constantly witnessed in practice. This example of theory is more inherent and innate rather than external

or overt at the theoretical end. It is done and lived, not talked about. The linkage is as pure as one might find anywhere.

5. The linkage to the thought, ideas, and teaching of Thomas Berry and Miriam Therese MacGillis is wide, although attitudes toward advertising that fact vary. For example, those communities more closely associated with an academic community have desired to be less obvious in making this connection (perhaps for fear of criticism by academics who are inherently more conservative and cautious). The latter situation is likely to change, however, with the increasing elevation of Thomas Berry, particularly, in academic circles, his substantial recognition by Harvard University and other major and elite academic institutions, and by increasing appreciation of the academically solid nature of Tom Berry's own intellectual background as a cultural historian, scholar of Eastern religions, philosopher of science, and "geologian."

6. Reading nature as revelation—from Tom Berry, Aquinas, the psalms, and many other sources—a return of the not very common attitude of seeing Nature as a book of revelation side by side with Holy Scripture, as complementary to one another.

There are undoubtedly more commonalties of theory yet to be discovered in these communities.

Commonalties of practice among these communities are everywhere to be found and quite numerous:

1. *Strawbale housing:* this particular housing form is extremely ecological in its nature; extremely low energy in its operation and its construction; very inexpensive; easily available to all in terms of expense and skills; socially just and viewed as a very exciting housing alternative for private residences, for retreat houses, for hermitages, and even for libraries, offices, community centers, and churches/chapels. Interest in strawbale housing and its technology is at a high level in almost all earth-centered religious communities, and actual examples exist, or are under construction at a surprisingly large number of such communities. Low intensive uses may be a little more common than high intensive uses but faith in them is strong. A strawbale house, through its low cost and accessibility/

availability, is socially just but it also meets favorably with just about every conceivable ecological principle (although perhaps ecologically stronger in the drier environments). Compost toilets as a method of solid waste treatment is also common as a parallel interest.

2. *Organic agricultural certification:* a serious goal if not always a reality for virtually all these communities, the members of which would often view chemical spray application (and chemical fertilizers) as an act of violence. Some communities are very purist seeking biodynamic or Demeter certification (after the teaching of Rudolph Steiner), others are content with state or soil association certification (Oregon Tilth, or NOFA, or other similar certification), and some are content (for the moment) with no actual certification but with meeting all or nearly all of the standards for certification. This too is virtually universal, and member Sisters are often active in organic certification organizations and movements. It is likely that such nuns have also been active in the debate over national organic certification standards.

3. *Community Supported Agriculture* (CSAs): the national CSA movement, now involving likely over two thousand farms nationwide (the actual number is not possible to know since there is no registration requirement) has caught on very strongly among women religious. The principle social and ecological values of CSA match almost perfectly the values of such communities, so this is very much a natural match. In addition, the CSA model, a shareholder model, is conducive to social justice concerns, to feeding the poor with the output of the farm. It is also coincident very strongly with organic agriculture, with the principles of ecology, and as a counter to the predominant and ethically questionable manner of obtaining food, governed by the cheapest price. (CSA constitutes a profound opportunity to achieve a very high level of integration of spirituality and nature, precisely the goal of both secular CSA and Sisters of Earth. CSA, within and outside these religious communities, is carried out both with and without animals.)

4. *Educational programming:* Most Sisters of Earth are educators at heart (with a few exceptions), and thus one expects to find a full slate of educational programming at most

communities. Invariably there is some type of newsletter periodical sent out to at least local area active participants; there is often an additional range of "light" literature on the community's activities, its positions on a wide variety of environmental and sometimes other issues (including agriculture), and sometimes shared stories/experiences. This educational programming would also include self-guided trail and tour literature, guided nature walks, farm tours, evening lectures, gatherings, sometimes the hosting of conferences, and, very often, weekend workshops. Videotapes are sometimes developed. Music can be a big part of these communities and tapes of their music and lectures are sometimes made. Courses may also be given occasionally with credit offered through local colleges.

5. *Energy conservation:* Some number of these communities grew philosophically from a time in the 1970s and early 1980s when energy and energy conservation were more important concerns than they have been in the years since. This concern and discussion has been continued in these communities. Likewise, knowledge of the ecological impacts of energy production and waste are very widely known, and thus the commitment to energy conservation in all its multitudinous forms is widespread and put into practice wherever possible. Energy wastage is clearly viewed as sinful. Climate change concerns in recent years have strengthened opposition to fossil fuel burning, adding to earlier strong antinuclear antipathies.

6. *Renewable energy:* There is a widely held belief that what energy is needed for the maintenance of life in the communities should be as much as possible, and often totally from renewable forms. Of the various renewable forms, two in particular have taken on a pivotal role: solar and wind. Most communities have seriously experimented with many types of solar energy, solar panels, photo voltaics, and so forth, as well as passive forms of solar, and are strong proponents of these energy types and their technologies. The affinity for wind energy in some of the communities is nothing less than extraordinary, with a real determination present to, in some cases, provide all of their electricity from wind or a combination of wind and solar. Biomass energy is part of the picture in some places. An emphasis on serious energy conservation

in combination with the alternative sources has meant a relatively small and clearly declining dependency on nuclear and fossil fuels, and other sources.

7. *Permaculture:* Many of the communities have active permaculture projects and many offer regular courses and workshops on this form of ecological agriculture and gardening. A link is made between gardening and landscape work and spiritual development. Many people who seek opportunity for enrollment in permaculture courses and who often have no other options in their region experience Sisters of Earth for the first time through these usually weekend or sometimes week-long courses.

8. *Biodynamic farming and gardening:* This form and its principles are becoming increasingly popular and commonplace in such communities. This is Steiner methodology (after Rudolph Steiner) and constitutes a very strong and disciplined form of organic agriculture, often going well beyond certification requirements.

9. *Celebration of solstices:* Part of the biodynamic or Steiner approach and very commonplace even in those Sisters of Earth communities not practicing biodynamic agriculture. Various rituals are developed and used. Some American Indian, some Christian and pre-Christian Celtic, perhaps other rituals are practiced at the seasonal changes.

10. *Internships:* There is often major dependency in these labor-intensive agricultural and land-based communities on volunteers and particularly on interns. Many communities increasingly have an organized internship program. Some cooperate with academic and other institutions to grant credit to interns toward diplomas, degrees, and certificates.

11. *Youth work, youth ministry, service education:* Related to internships but more oriented to service to others rather than self-education, youth are frequently involved in working on the land in the Sisters of Earth communities as part of ministry and/or service responsibilities, sometimes in connection with Christian Confirmation classes, Sunday School classes, social service obligations of both church-related and secular high schools and various youth organizations. Sisters of Earth communities always have labor needs and always

provide productive, tangible and, to many, personally rewarding opportunities for service.

12. *Ritual:* All Sisters of Earth communities are involved in prayer in many forms, in the conduct of work as prayer, and in the conduct of many creation-based and earth-based rituals, especially around the solstice and equinox periods, the change of seasons, and in connection with the feast of the patron saint of ecology, Saint Francis of Assisi (October 4), and at other times. The monastic communities are even more involved with ritual associated with recognition of the hours (time of day). Sisters of Earth communities also conduct integrated American Indian/Native American ritual with Christian ritual, develop ecologically based ritual, and sometimes conduct Eastern philosophic ritual, all in recognition of the value of ritual in developing and fostering an earth-based or creation spirituality.

13. *Retreat, Hermitage:* Virtually all Sisters of Earth communities provide opportunity for guided and nonguided spiritual retreats, both Christian and non-Christian, and usually contain retreat houses (sometimes of strawbale construction), retreat-oriented (and also non-retreat oriented) trail networks, and so forth, and a general atmosphere supportive of contemplation. All of these experiences are earth and creation-based. Some Sisters of Earth communities also provide more isolated hermitage opportunities for those who wish to be totally separated from other people for periods of time. Contemplation with nature and creation is the idea.

14. *Ecological restoration:* Restoration of various natural ecosystems (woodland, wetlands, prairie, etc.) is an increasingly common activity in Sisters of Earth communities (especially those that are academically a part of, or closely affiliated with a college or university which can provide guidance and technical assistance to carry out such work, and also college student and other student labor to perform the work). This is a strong scientific and technical link to the Creation and is done as both science and prayer. It is less common in communities not academically attached or affiliated, although the climate of support and interest is present in such communities as well, held back only by a lack of means. It is likely that ecological restoration may become a much more significant aspect of Sisters of Earth communities in the future.

15. *Cooperative Extension:* Sisters of Earth communities are now increasingly turning to one another for technical assistance in agriculture, land management, and ecosystem restoration rather than to government and university cooperative extension services, mainly out of shared common values and a common rejection of many of the values represented by the public cooperative extension services (corporate, industrial, chemical, large-scale, energy-intensive, commodity production orientation, etc.). Additionally, Sisters of Earth communities are increasingly being called upon to provide assistance to the public and to secular organizations in their areas as the public cooperative extension services increasingly find themselves unable to serve the values represented by the Sisters of Earth communities. A most interesting question: Can Sisters of Earth communities become a significant Cooperative Extension Service for one another, largely supplanting the respective State Cooperative Extension Services? Also, can these communities become a significant source of expertise for their own regions and neighborhoods?

16. *Living machines:* Interest in establishing living machines from wastewater (including but not limited to gray water) is increasing, following John Todd and Thomas Berry thinking, combined with composting of all organics on site.

17. *Meditation:* Labyrinth medieval walking prayer and meditation rituals (often modeled after Chartres Cathedral in France) are increasingly being developed at these sites, as is the Cosmic Walk model and ritual. Both forms of meditation are used with the development of site guides to sites of special spirituality on the property.

18. *Teaching organic agriculture:* There is an increasing ability and practice of Sisters of Earth to teach organic agriculture both to other communities among Sisters and also and especially to other people (neighbors) in their regions who may have no other source for information.

19. *Senior citizen/retiree housing:* Frequently present due to the advanced age of many of the retired nuns in the Motherhouses, and also the great external societal need for the aging population nationwide. Sometimes on-site are only Sisters, sometimes both Sisters and lay people from outside the community. Presence of these facilities and people can mean a

market for garden produce and a source of labor and assistance of many kinds. It is also a source for compost and wastewater, both of which can be used as farm inputs.

20. *Labor:* Occasionally, there is opportunity to use penal labor (juvenile offenders, honor farm, low-security prisoners, and, very infrequently, high-security prisoners); and to also use Boy and Girl Scouts fulfilling scout project obligations.

21. *Immigrants:* New immigrants of diverse ethnic groups, together with the presence of local people in need can be the base for contract gardens for those who have no other gardening possibility (local inner-city people)—varying ethnicities can enhance these opportunities; developed at Mankato, Minnesota, and soon elsewhere.

22. *Roles:* Training opportunities and roles for lay parish ministers in eco-spirituality, eco-justice, ecology and religion, and food and farm issues—Mankato is doing it, perhaps others, and many more can follow.

23. *World experience:* International and intercultural backgrounds of Sisters who frequently have considerable Third World experience relates to broadened outlook, sources of external cultural knowledge, and so forth, at many Sisters of Earth communities, communities which become far more internationalized and internationally capable of assisting immigrants than might otherwise be the case.

Three Sisters of Earth communities, Heartland Farm in Kansas, Prairiewoods in Iowa, and Michaela Farm in Indiana, have already been described in detail in chapter three on "Outstanding Community Models of Sustainability." There are, however, many more examples of such communities, and there is much we can learn from these models.

ST. MARY-OF-THE-WOODS, INDIANA

The St. Mary-of-the-Woods community in Indiana, located in the college community and campus of the same name, has two components: a nationally operated master's degree program in Earth Literacy, based strongly on Thomas Berry's New Story and his thought; and the White Violet Center for Eco-Justice. The Sisters of St. Joseph (SSJs), to which the

Director of the Graduate Degree Program in Earth Literacy, Sr. Mary Lou Dolan, a longtime college professor and biologist, belongs, have a stated environmental ethic but no land and little opportunity for environmental practice. Sr. Mary Lou's Earth Literacy program (with twenty-two students, mainly women, and half members of religious orders), has a strong connection to the Dominicans' Genesis Farm in New Jersey and to Genesis Farm founder Sr. Miriam Therese MacGillis.[14] Indeed, the MacGillis and closely related Berry influence are found throughout the program. The White Violet Center on the campus is a project of the Sisters of Providence, operators of the college and an order with a long history of land-based sustainable activity, a strong land ethic, and a history of issuing earth spirituality statements. Given that this is a college campus setting, there has been some reservation in dealings with the college faculty, and particularly science faculty, in overtly using the work of Thomas Berry, given the challenge Berry represents to the Cartesian/Newtonian reductionistic scientific mind. Other Catholic college campuses that have hosted these Sisters of Earth communities have had some similar experiences, although such attitudes will change over time. On the other hand, the presence of the college community, the technical expertise of its faculty, and the expertise and energy of students, as interns or as researchers, has meant that White Violet and St. Mary-of-the-Woods have been able to sponsor ecological restoration projects as an important part of their ecological studies and eco-spiritual ministry, an important activity which is often impossible, or at least very difficult in nonacademic settings. Overall in the range of the Sisters of Earth activities, there is typically, and here as well, very strong female participation, religious and lay, and only weak male participation.

The White Violet Center for Eco-Justice is only peripherally related to the college and its curriculum, most directly through student interns (which represents great potential for the Center).[15] There are also good potential connections to the long history of sustainable land-based heritage of the religious order which founded and owns the institution and its land. The presence of the graduate program in Earth Literacy has the further potential for marketing among graduating seniors, if focused right, and if examples of students in the program are put forth as models for the undergraduates. Internships and ecological restoration is a further linkage to the undergraduate students at the college.

In addition to ecological restoration, White Violet's program involves a CSA, small farm, some ecological building design, and a program of instruction (short courses), weekend workshops, newsletter, and so forth, in ecological living; in permaculture and in ecological design, with an emphasis on the justice and moral choice components of this way of life. It also features a strawbale retreat house, a herd of alpacas explicitly to support the organic agriculture, an organized education program, wetlands restoration, and social advocacy. Their mission is to foster a way of living that recognizes the interdependence of all creation. They are governed in all of their work by the twin Sisters of Providence charisms of hope and healing.

MARIANIST ENVIRONMENTAL EDUCATION CENTER (BERGAMO CENTER), OHIO

Another college campus-based program, one with a very large-scale emphasis on ecological restoration, is the Marianist Environmental Education Center at the University of Dayton, an old and well-established Catholic university with considerable land acreage in and around Dayton, Ohio. Consequently, a number of students are involved through both internships and service projects, as are faculty through teaching and research. As with St. Mary-of-the-Woods, this program is not an academic program of the university but rather a service effort of a women's religious order, the Marianists. The effort here is very much into science-based ecological restoration on 130 acres of woodland, prairie (some of the easternmost in the United States), and wetlands, which effort includes a strong focus on native plants and all that that represents, a very labor intensive activity.[16] The religious community and lay assistants are so focused on their restoration work that they are, in fact, becoming a model for ecological restoration, and they even host academic meetings on this subject. In its work, the community fulfills many local area requests for nature education, for Church confirmation classes, and for service learning opportunity. They serve the needs of many students, both high school, university, and retreatants; their programs are very interactive and work-oriented. They bring forward a very high integration of art, sculpture, landscaping, and ritual with native plants, with the goal of a true integration of spirit and nature. A Marianist brother who is also a university professor of biology, Br. Don Geiger, S.M., a protégé of Thomas Berry, is a key figure in aiding this program and in giving it a high degree of scientific credibility. This community uses its college base well, is perhaps a little more Catholic and less ecumenical than others (due to its Catholic college connection), and has potential for more public recognition than other such communities. It is a ministry which the Marianist order, nationwide, both men and women, are aware of and proud of. There is a better gender balance, with the participation of some number of males who are absent or nearly so from so many other Sisters of Earth projects.

VILLA MARIA, PENNSYLVANIA

The large Villa Maria community and motherhouse of the Sisters of the Humility of Mary in western Pennsylvania on the Ohio state line, constitute a large resource base of farm, forest and pasture land and a more than a century-old and strong agricultural heritage. In fact, the ecological and eco-justice approach of this community starts from agriculture at its base. These Sisters are into permaculture, and their operations are all organic.[17] (They have an on-site market for feeding the large motherhouse community for 75 percent of their crop of vegetables. However, a very substantial quantity of their farm product totaling many thousands of pounds, goes to outreach programs such as city rescue missions and the Salvation Army in large and small cities in Ohio and Pennsylvania, for produce for the poor is their centerpiece.) Because the crop is all claimed, they have no CSA but are interested in the idea. The Sisters have plenty of tillable acreage, livestock, gardens, and four hundred acres under a forestry stewardship program. They use compost from the livestock, sponsor rotational grazing workshops using the Holistic Resource Management model of HRM, have constructed strawbale housing for retreatants and for a hermitage, and an "art house" for display of painting and sculpture, with an herb garden and a Zen room for meditation. They have a full program of classes and workshops on land-based and other eco-spirituality, and eco-justice topics, instruction in how (and why) to live ecologically and sustainably, and very detailed Master Plans (essentially Green Plans) for future direction and development. The Villa Maria community is proof that large-scale agriculture is possible in the East in these settings. They also have such high commitment to the serious raising of food for the poor and hungry that this place could qualify for the social justice chapter of this volume (even though that is not its origin); the insistence on organic/ecological agriculture places it squarely in the eco-spirituality realm. There is strong openness to Thomas Berry and particularly strong inspiration from the Dominican Sr. Miriam Therese MacGillis.

There is a strong realization, much like at Michaela Farm and other such women's religious communities, that the Sisters of Earth movement is now so strong that it can supplant some of the role of government, particularly the role of the Cooperative Extension Service, especially given the inherent long-term weakness of the Cooperative Extension Service and land grant colleges of agriculture when it comes to ecological agriculture in practice and the theory behind it.

CENTER FOR EARTH SPIRITUALITY AND RURAL MINISTRY, MINNESOTA

The Center for Earth Spirituality and Rural Ministry at Mankato in southern Minnesota is a project of the School Sisters of Notre Dame. This particular community is especially activist in matters pertaining to the land grant university (University of Minnesota), with state government, with statewide sustainable agriculture organizations, with local agricultural cooperative experiment station units, with local CSAs, and with organic agriculture regulations and certification.[18] This community, a Sisters motherhouse, is very agriculturally oriented with a strong belief in the culture of agriculture, and a strong belief in animals as having a necessary role in agriculture. Once again, here is a community very influenced by Thomas Berry, especially in their path toward activism. Given their statewide activist focus, these Notre Dame Sisters are less overtly involved with Sisters of Earth and a little less involved on-site on their 150 acres than they might be otherwise. But they do have projects on the land.

The School Sisters of Notre Dame have a long-term rural life committee, and many years of connection to the National Catholic Rural Life Conference. The work of their Rural Life Committee is all related to food and agriculture and is strongly supported by the order which has adopted a strong Care for the Earth statement and issues regular statements on this subject. The philosophy of this order stems from social justice mandates of Catholicism but carries them further. If we don't care for the Earth, then we don't care for the poor, because they're connected: this is the essence of their rationale. Their new Earth Committee has a strong ministry to rural people and rural community.

On their own land in Mankato, the School Sisters sponsor prairie restoration in two areas and an oak-savanna restoration (in spite of the lack of presence of an academic community to assist). They have established a Conservation Reserve Program (CRP) to return former cropland to natural vegetation and have removed this land from farm lease. They are introducing the new concept of "contract gardens" for both immigrant communities in Mankato, and for others in need. These "contract gardens" reflect the diverse ethnicities of people from four continents in their design, operation, and resultant crops. They've developed a "site guide" to spiritual sites on the "hill" (their land), a guide not only strongly linked to ecology, agriculture, and history, but also largely serving their own resident community (a common practice in Sisters of Earth communities). They also actively manage forest and woodland to reduce erosion and eliminate exotic species. There are some limited efforts at buildings, including low flush and compost toilets, and energy saving light bulbs, but they are not especially oriented to the built environment. Externally, they are very involved in WISA (Women in Sustainable Agriculture); in assisting in the development of CSAs in their region; in supporting rural parish communities by producing eco-spiritual materials for them; organizing diocesan celebrations related to land-agriculture-ecology; pastoral ministry programs to lay ministry in the diocese, and some ecumenically to Protestant denominations, especially to the Presbyterian Church. They have much involvement with the Minnesota-based Land Stewardship Project and the Minnesota Food Association. They are active in the River Sabbath Team, an ecumenical group on the Minnesota River in Mankato. They clearly connect their order's charism to impoverishment of the Earth and the integrity of creation. Overall, they devote a third of their time to on-site efforts (piecemeal, without a master plan), a third to external social ministry in the parishes, and a third to political ministry (largely statewide land and agriculture issues).

The thinking and resultant work here at Mankato long precedes Thomas Berry and the Sisters of Earth movement, but has been inspired, strengthened, and furthered by it. The emphasis on agriculture, food, rural community involvement, and the plight of the small farmer is central, though strongly allied with both ecology and spirituality, revealing the culture of the area and that of the two founders who still direct the organization. The emphasis on external political activism reflects both strong tradition in the region and the nature of the Center's leadership. The three-directional thrust is somewhat different from many Sisters of Earth communities and reduces attention somewhat to the immediate site. The gardens, barn restoration for retreatants, an arts center, and designation of "sacred sites" ecologically based is very much in keeping with other Sisters of Earth efforts. On the other hand, the link to the rural poor and to the farm crisis are stronger here than in Sisters of Earth communities elsewhere. The Center is very ecumenical in its ministry and politically liberal. "Contract gardens" and involvement with immigrant ethnicities in gardening might well be a very exportable idea to other ecojustice religious communities.

SINSINAWA—CHURCHES CENTER FOR LAND AND PEOPLE, WISCONSIN

In the extreme southwest corner of Wisconsin, bordering Illinois and Iowa, lies the great Sinsinawa Mound on top of which lies the large Dominican motherhouse of Sinsinawa, and one of the earlier Dominican Sisters of Earth communities. This is the base of agricultural and ecological activist Sr. Miriam Brown. Sinsinawa itself was for more than a century a major farming operation, crops, livestock, fruit and dairy in a rich agricultural region. Experiencing the so typical move away from the culture of agriculture in the 1960s and 1970s, Sinsinawa saw an agro-ecological resurgence in the late 1980s and 1990s under Sr. Miriam's capable hands. But, again typical of too many communities and their sound ecological efforts, with leadership change at the top, how does one keep a sustainability project sustainable? Good progress was reversed and Sr. Miriam's external agricultural activist programs continued while much on-site did not. Sinsinawa remains headquarters for the ecumenical and important Churches Center for Land and People, an early activist organization staking out a clear role for all Christian churches in ecological and small-scale agriculture, land stewardship, and the serious questions of moral choice surrounding both.[19] The Sinsinawa site has woodlands, orchards, vegetable gardens, an oak-prairie-savanna ecological restoration project from former pasture lands, prairie wildflower restoration, croplands, streams, and apple production (close to organic, with close cooperation with the University of Wisconsin College of Agriculture on insect trapping in order to better time and reduce the chemical sprays). Crops are alfalfa, hay, and corn in rotation, all for dairy cow feed. The beef cattle herd is gone, as are poultry and hogs. There is no harvest or management of the woodlands (sugar maple-oak association), while dogwoods, other hardwoods, and evergreens are being planted to counter serious stream erosion problems which have been unattended for far too long. Grapes are raised for jelly and wine. Leaves are collected for mulch and both vegetable gardens are large. There is serious discussion of wind energy for this site, and a possible wind energy/solar energy complementarity, but no serious long-term planning for land use, energy, or food has been done. There is a consciousness here of eco-spirituality (further attested to by the strong on-site bookstore selection of titles in this area), and of energy and eco-agricultural matters, but the will to act is much more questionable. What is not in question is the off-site external will to act of the Churches Center for Land and People (CCLP), and thus the Sinsinawa site becomes a major base of eco-spiritual inspiration and church connection to ecological agriculture, while not necessarily demonstrating these beliefs through action on this site today. CCLP and its founder-director and board are clearly strong in their knowledge of and commitment to ecological thought and eco-spirituality, in theory and in practice. Their own literature and their activity attests to this. Whether or not CCLP's three-part thrust into land stewardship, spirituality, and ethics will be as successful in inspiring Sinsinawa's changing leadership to follow suit at their beautiful Sinsinawa Mound remains to be seen.

SISTERS OF ST. JOSEPH OF NAZARETH ECOSPIRITUALITY CENTER, MICHIGAN

The 270-acre farm and the 85-acre motherhouse of the Sisters of St. Joseph of Nazareth Ecospirituality Center near Kalamazoo, Michigan constitutes another very active Sisters of Earth community.[20] Herein lies another community in the embrace of Thomas Berry's thought and action. The farm is certified organic, largely in the Conservation Reserve Program (CRP), and has both cropland and a woodland. The motherhouse property includes fifty-five acres of marsh, fields, and woods, with extensive boardwalks and raised trails built throughout the marsh. A conservation plan for the farmland has been completed, and a full energy and eco-audit has been carried out by Fr. Al Fritsch's ecological assessment team, both indicators of serious intent by the Sisters. The Sisters are seeking to form a farmland trust for the farm itself with the Southwest Michigan Conservancy, a move which would protect the land for farming. There are a number of woodlot management studies completed, and a detailed plan for the establishment of a future eco-village on the site, a village with many advanced energy and building designs to maximize energy conservation and ecologically sensitive living. This village would be an eco-spiritual community for forty families. The project would be facilitated by the Sisters but separately incorporated so that the residents would share ownership and direction.

Importantly, all of these efforts are strongly linked to the reconciliation charisms of the Sisters of St. Joseph of Nazareth, an order founded in 1650. Reconciliation here means humans' reconciliation with Earth, with the planet, and with the Creator of all through the Creation, as well as the more traditional reconciliation between and among humans, and reconciliation with God. Ecological living can be seen in a secular vein as living in reconciliation with, as well as in harmony with, the ecosystem.

This project of the Sisters of St. Joseph of Nazareth is ecologically excellent conceptually but is largely a one woman show, the effort of Sr. Ginny Jones, with a small amount of assistance from laypersons. There being only one religious significantly involved, the idea of religious community leadership becomes a little questionable. However, Sr. Ginny is well networked with the Sisters of Earth and has been so for a long time. She is very advanced on ecological, eco-spiritual, and alternative energy knowledge, and on agriculture and agro-ecology. She has excellent links to the National Catholic Rural Life Conference, which holds her in high regard, to diocesan and other church people, both in other Catholic orders and ecumenically, and to the scientific community (she herself is a biologist), and to the most state-of-the-art thinking needed for success in this area. She has the sound support (if not more active participation) of her own order. She has significant responsibility and authority for what she is doing and is both ambitious and visionary. The potential of her work at Kalamazoo is enormous and, if successful, will undoubtedly be widely emulated.

DOMINICAN EARTH PROJECT, KENTUCKY

The Dominican Earth Project at St. Catharine's in central Kentucky, known formally as the Office of Earth Education and Sustainable Living, is another of the communities inspired by the work of Sr. Miriam Therese MacGillis.[21] Under the able leadership of Sr. Rose Cummins, O.P., this project uniquely blends a college, the College of St. Catharine, with its undergraduate enrollment and unusual (for a Catholic or any private institution) agricultural teaching program, with a Dominican Motherhouse and extensive farm acreage in a rural and essentially non-Catholic area of the mid-south. Potential exists, therefore, to blend college faculty, college students, and sustainable agriculture and gardening efforts with the idealism and passionate commitment of the Dominican Sisters on the site, to mold their Dominican charism with ecology which, here in particular, can play out in conjunction with a collegiate academic program and an agricultural and rural community heritage. The nearby farm of Wendell Berry and the popularity of his writings and influence in the local area are an added and unique resource to support the success of this endeavor. The project is currently known for adult earth education workshops each spring and fall; earth education with school age children; celebrations of the turning of the seasons; provision of an "Earth Alert" column for three local newspapers; two energy-efficient retreat cabins out on the farm pastures (with more planned); maintenance of a woodland trail and retreat site; organic gardens (including one for and by local immigrant Mexican children); and a new recycling center. Seven acres of former pastureland have been set aside to model simple and sustainable living, on a site called "Jonquil Ridge." Many workshops and noncredit classes round out the offerings, and the atmosphere of these endeavors complements the new college interdisciplinary academic program in ecology and citizenship studies. A detailed ten-year plan has been drawn for the Dominican Earth Project, under a mission statement which identifies the project as "a model ecological learning center, committed to earth literacy, earth spirituality, and sustainable living." The statement also remarks: "Aware of the interconnectedness of all God's creation, we open ourselves to the wisdom of the universe," a very Thomas Berryesque approach.[22]

Finally, this Dominican Office of Earth Education and Sustainable Living also hosts, on a regular basis, meetings of the Ursuline, Sisters of Charity and Loretto, Mercy, Providence, and Dominican Sisters earth literacy network, indicating a strong degree of involvement in the nationwide Sisters of Earth Network.

GENESIS FARM, NEW JERSEY

No study of Sisters of Earth communities would be complete without acknowledgement of the mother of all such communities—Sr. Miriam Therese MacGillis' Genesis Farm in New Jersey.[23] Genesis Farm is essentially the flagship of the chain of Dominican women's eco-spiritual communities extending from Massachusetts to Kansas, and Sr. Miriam, outstanding spokesperson for the movement and a major inspiration to many, is the founder and director. Genesis Farm has provided a model for the Franciscans, Sisters of Charity, Sisters of Loretto, Sisters of Notre Dame, and numerous other Catholic women's religious orders in their design and organization of what now constitutes the Sisters of Earth network. [All the pieces are there at Genesis Farm: a major community supported agriculture (CSA) project, drawing from a market area which even includes New York City; organic farm certification or close to it; extensive strawbale construction for housing and offices; great attention to energy conservation and to alternative renewable energy sources; great attention to the health of the soil and to ecological principles; good labor sources (in Genesis Farm's case, from correctional institutions, even higher security penal institutions); a sound and extensive informal education program (workshops, classes, seminars year-round—even on such subjects as vegetarian cooking); and a formal one as well (graduate degree program in Earth Literacy, similar to the one at St. Mary-of-the-Woods); early involvement in permaculture training; wholistic resource management on the land; explicit connection to the Dominican charism and to Catholic social teaching; and extraordinarily direct and strong inspiration from and involvement of Thomas Berry, even to the extent that Sr. Miriam Therese could be viewed as an important interpreter of Thomas Berry and his thought to women religious, to women, and to our society in general.] Genesis Farm refers to itself as a learning center for reinhabiting the Earth, giving it as broad a scope as anyone could imagine. Learning and learning by doing are the key, as per the Dominican mission, whether in the Ecological Learning Center, in informal or formal education programs, or out on the 140 acres of the farm, croplands, and associated woodlands. Genesis Farm takes seriously its "exploration of the Sacred Universe," and its need to be a serious and primary teacher in the art of living simply.

Crystal Spring at Plainville, Massachusetts, Crown Point and Shepherd's Corner in Ohio, St. Catherine of Siena in Kentucky, Sparkill in New York, and the already noted Heartland Farm in Kansas and Sinsinawa in Wisconsin have followed the inspiration of Genesis Farm, as will undoubtedly the new Dominican development, Rosaryville, in Louisiana.

One shouldn't be surprised to see the Franciscan women equally active, from the already mentioned Michaela Farm in Indiana and Prairiewoods in Iowa to the Sisters of St. Francis communities in Sylvania and Tiffin, Ohio, and Clinton and Dubuque in Iowa, Rochester and Annandale in Minnesota, and Osseo in Wisconsin, among other places. The Sisters of Loretto in St. Louis, Missouri, with communities in a number of states and regions, are strongly involved in this work philosophically, publish a newsletter, and organize meetings and conferences, albeit with perhaps less direct involvement on the land. The Sisters of Notre Dame have their Cuvilly Farm and Cuvilly Arts and Earth Center in Massachusetts, a pioneer in CSA in its area. The Sisters of Charity have their ecological activities in the Upper Mississippi Valley of Iowa, in Ohio and in New Jersey and elsewhere, while the Sisters of Mercy are also ecologically active in the Midwest, in Maine and elsewhere.

EARTH CONNECTION, OHIO

Earth Connection near Cincinnati, Ohio is a reminder that not all of these communities which are about sustainability are themselves sustainable. After a trial period of support from the broader religious community of which it is a part, Earth Connection was no longer able to sustain itself and has closed its doors. Nevertheless, Earth Connection has something to teach us.

The outstanding work of Sister of Charity Paula Gonzales of Cincinnati, Ohio and her Earth Connection organization do deserve particular mention here. Sr. Paula's dedication to recycling of ALL materials and to extremely strong energy conservation are nearly legendary around the country, and her extensive community home of recycled materials near the Ohio River is visited by many. Her speaking and writing on these subjects are known nationwide, all based on her spirituality-ecology connection through her Sisters of Charity charism. The centerpiece of her work is to replace fossil fuel and nuclear energy as rapidly as possible. In 1981, she built her "house of the sun," a former chicken coop converted through solar energy and recycling into a large and attractive home that operates on very little energy, and that is mainly passive solar with super insulation. The institutionalization of Sr. Paula's work was Earth Connection, a center for living and reflection about living lightly on the Earth. And today Sr. Paula's involvement in championing wind energy is as strong and as passionate as are her decades of work on solar energy and energy conservation. Her effort in southern Ohio has been a one person Sister of Earth eco-spiritual community and has attracted much more public attention than do most other communities discussed in this chapter.

Many other orders could be added to this list. While all regions of the United States are represented in these endeavors, the Midwest continues to be the strongest of the regions in Sisters of Earth representation. Mention should be made of the influence of Sisters of Earth on the women's monastic communities, including the well-publicized forest management activities of the Benedictines at the Monastery of St. Gertrude in Idaho, the garden and nature activities and educational programs at the Benedictine Monastery of St. Scholastica in Oregon, the Carmelite women and men in Colorado, the Trappist men in Utah, the Passionist women and men (Thomas Berry's order) in Ontario, Canada, the Passionists historically at St. Gabriel's in Pennsylvania, the Benedictine women of Mt. St. Benedict in far northwest Minnesota, and others elsewhere. These projects vary in size but all are making a mark, quietly and effectively, and all are demonstrating the effectiveness of the merger of ecological thought with monastic rules, with the charisms of numerous different orders on the land in a variety of places, with Catholic social teaching, with Christianity, with faith and with spirituality. The impact of this movement is likely well beyond the small size and quiet, humble nature of its participants, leaders, and architects. And the movement as a whole is a strong testament to the critical and foundational role of women, women in community, women on the land, women engaged with the sacrality of the Creation. Often times the women in question are highly seasoned and courageous individuals who have faced enormous hardship, even the risk of losing their lives, working in Asia, Africa, and Latin America. And consequently they do not tremble in the face of opposition and obstacles to what they consider their life work, their role in life. The marriage of their interpretation of ecological imperative and their conviction of faith imperative is potent. Thomas Berry and his thinking have played no small role as a catalyst in this process during the last few decades.

As we have seen, the way to achieve environmental sustainability is through ecological living. The way to achieve ecological living is ultimately through spirituality, since the changeover to ecological living requires a conversion away from the dominant paradigm or value system of our culture, and the development of resistance to that value system. It requires rejection of that value system, rejection of consumption and waste as a lifestyle, and the embrace of frugality as a core principle.

We might posit the question facing us this way:

- If we are to survive, we must. . . .

- If our children, our grandchildren, are to survive, they must. . . .

- As faith believers, if we are to achieve eternal salvation, we must. . . .

- The answer undoubtedly is "do things sustainably." But how?

A significant portion of the answer to that question is what we are learning from the many Sisters of Earth community models presented to us in this chapter. When we put these lessons together with their underlying philosophy, we might conclude that one could live in a sustainable setting which would include, as indicators of its own sustainability:

- *a strawbale passive solar house with solar hot water that would require no or very little heat in winter nor air conditioning in summer;*

- *active solar in higher sunshine areas with photo-voltaics for storage, electricity provided by the photo-voltaics, perhaps with wind power, depending on the site;*

- *active wind power from turbines on-site, with storage capability and with electricity sales back to the utility, ideally with reverse metering, if the site remains on the power grid;*

- *active integration of wind and solar energy to maximize their complementarity;*

- *radiant heat in the floors on all new and renovated construction (from solar power);*

- *gray water system and roof and gutter cisterns to provide watering of gardens, trees, shrubs, and so forth;*

- *constructed wetlands for blackwater (sewage) disposal;*

- *laundry drying on outdoor lines or, in cold or wet season, near woodstoves, and complete avoidance of electric clothes dryers;*

- *wood stoves, as appropriate, and wood pellet stoves in some areas, with some pellet transport, as necessary;*

- *highly energy efficient appliances of high quality, which amortize their upfront cost through their long life span;*

- *reduction in usage of all heat generating appliances (i.e., clothes dryers, etc.);*

- *composting toilets and low water toilets;*

- *composting of all garden and yard waste, and all household organics;*

- *no built-in garbage disposal;*

- *reduction of private motor vehicle usage to the extent possible, with maximazation of alternative transport systems (i.e., car pooling, public transit, bicycling, walking, reducing or eliminating less necessary travel);*

- *permaculture; kitchen gardens; larger food gardens; farms (with and without livestock); sponsorship of CSAs; membership (shareholding) in CSAs; direct food purchase from local farmers; support of farmers markets; co-sponsorship of area farmers markets; satisfying as many food needs as possible from the local area; avoidance of large corporate/industrial food sources such as food clubs, chain supermarkets, and so forth; use of community kitchens (as well as sponsorship and construction of such kitchens) for food canning, storage, preparation, and processing; involvement in and support of local agricultural cooperatives; support and growth of native species as much as possible;*

- *practice of the principles of Holistic Resource Management (HRM), with livestock and in other ways;*

- *expect to pay a fair price for food, knowing that a fair price is not necessarily the lowest price, and is likely more than mass market competition;*

- *choose and support certified organic, low or no chemical, and low-energy input systems;*

- *support LOCAL farmers as a first priority, even over organic;*

- *eat lower on the food chain, reducing meat consumption to a few times per week, or eliminate meat from the diet, as desired;*

- *support local business, so that local business is there to support us;*

- *form local community, local network, and broader network for support in all of these practices, perhaps using e-mail technology to assist communication and networking.*

If on a farm or ranch, for sustainable farming, ranching, living, one would add:

- *placing top priority on the soil: if you take care of the soil, the soil will take care of you; likewise, if you take care of the range, the range will take care of the animals and you;*

- *diversification in farming and diversification in use of land is critical, just as is biodiversity in natural systems;*

- *use of Holistic Resource Management (HRM) is important, as are all aspects of rotation (and, as well, free-range chickens, chicken tractors, pasture pigs, use of goats, donkeys, and other highly efficient animals which give good return (e.g., goats produce meat, milk, cheese, soap and fertilizer, and hides, as well as keeping under control certain undesirable or otherwise unusable forage plants—a tremendous return on a small investment);*

- *full integration of livestock (grazing, fertilizer, diversity) into the life of the farm;*

- *seed saving and using heirloom varieties, supporting seed banks, contributing to seed banks, and so forth.*

All of these systems are in broad and common usage and constitute standard practice in the Sisters of Earth and monastic communities described in this volume. Some of them are so universal that, upon arrival in such a community, one might ask, Where is your strawbale structure? Where are your compost piles? Where are your organic gardens?—and expect to be led to them. All of the techniques are good, sound, and secular environmental conservation techniques, and good agricultural practice. But they are, by today's standards, outside the contemporary culture. That is where spirituality, faith if you will, enter the picture.

Faith belief provides a way to view this work thus far. All these measures which appear to be small, and perhaps relatively unsuccessful and unsustainable at the moment, will come into their own when circumstances and the times require it. It's a matter of being ready for that time, of preparing for it. All of these techniques, therefore, and, as well, their further refinement and evolution, will come into their own.

THE FOUNDATIONAL WORK OF ALBERT FRITSCH OF KENTUCKY

No treatment of Sisters of Earth communities, churches, and religious communities on the land, of faith-based land stewardship or of land-based eco-spirituality would be complete without mention of the pioneering and foundational work of Jesuit priest, environmental scientist, and ecological ethicist Albert Fritsch of Kentucky. While the presence and ecological/eco-spiritual work of religious communities on the land has been almost exclusively the work of women, women's religious communities, women's monastic communities, the foundational work of two men, both religious, both Catholic priests, one a monk, cannot be underestimated. It is in so many ways central. One, Thomas Berry, we have already met. The other is an environmental scientist and appropriate technologist, Albert Fritsch. One, Thomas Berry, is philosophical and theoretical. The other, Albert Fritsch, although himself an important ethicist and philosopher, is as hands-on, applied, practical, and, I might add, as activist, as one could possibly be.

Al Fritsch worked for a decade with Ralph Nader in Washington on energy and appropriate technology questions nationally, before returning to his native Kentucky to apply what he had learned at the community level and in aid of Appalachian people with limited opportunity and income. A hands-on, no-nonsense activist in every sense, much of Al's work is based in ecological auditing and assessment (the latter of which Al equates with spiritual direction). Al applied himself to the development of a host of appropriate small-scale and intermediate-scale technologies in every area of housing design and construction, energy conservation, and alternative energy development at the home and small community scale, organic gardening for serious food provision, food processing, preparation, storage, and forest and woodland management. He has authored and coauthored numerous technical publications (which he has also published) in all of these areas, obtainable at low cost and available to all (in addition to his widely known ecological ethics books and articles). He has also made corresponding videotapes (and broadcast them regularly on community TV), organized numerous conferences and gatherings of both a hands-on and a philosophical nature, and he produces a regular newsletter and a popular calendar of simplicity practice in daily life. All these things he has achieved under the auspices of his two decade-old Appalachia-Science in the Public Interest (ASPI), a private nonprofit organization under Al's leadership, which precisely practices what it preaches to others in every way, which walks its talk and challenges others to do likewise. But alongside this important work, Al has organized and recently spun off his very successful and nationally known Resource Assessment Service (RAS), a group designed to accomplish energy and ecological audits, indoors and outdoors, on properties in many of the U.S. states in all regions. What are these properties? They are the churches, homes, retreat centers, monasteries and associated properties, farms, forests, pastures of Catholic religious orders throughout the country. Interestingly, almost all this work has been contracted by women's communities, including most of the Sisters of Earth communities and many of the monasteries described in this volume. In his ministry, Al has observed that, while individual men religious may have very strong interest in and commitment toward ecological living and eco-spirituality, it is almost never the case that a community of men has such interest or commitment in these matters. It is much more common for most or all of the women in a religious community to be committed in this way. With RAS Al and his team became intimately familiar with the problems and challenges facing land-owning religious communities, and, as well, their responses to them across the nation. Al was very early, therefore, connected to the Sisters of Earth communities, and other communities of women religious in a very intimate way. This led him to assist these communities in the important act of cross-fertilization and helped them greatly (as all would agree) in becoming solidly grounded in this endeavor. This work also enabled Al not only to organize highly successful meetings and conferences, but also to publish in ways that would explicitly serve and encourage them. Albert Fritsch's belief is that all of these communities have a serious moral obligation toward the land and toward sustainable living, to the honoring of ecological principles, an obligation stemming from their Christian faith and, as well, from the particular charism of their order. This moral obligation goes well beyond any obligation they might have to be good citizens, or even to model ecological living and good land stewardship, as important as that might be. It is far more important to recycle, to steward the land well, to do no harm to the Creation, out of a Christian sense of the love of God and the sacrality of God's creation, than to do any of these things for any earthly purpose. The spiritual connection in these matters is, therefore, crucial. To do, to act, and to understand the spiritual connection to that action are necessary. Al has said the activists are the ones who articulate a Christian spirituality—not "thinkers." Early in his work, Al Fritsch observed, with respect to women's eco-spirituality, that the women involved are doers, not talkers, and that they don't talk about their work, nor do others, so it's easy for a person not to have any awareness of their existence. Al has found that the women's religious communities are much more open to living ecologically, to energy conservation, to living sustainably, than are men's. Men talk, women do, he tells us. Al Fritsch also finds that many women religious are not initially influenced by Thomas Berry but carry a natural intuition that something is wrong and that their nurturance capabilities demands that they work to heal. Al believes, however, that they are much encouraged by Thomas Berry—this suggests a greater depth in what these women are about. A possible further insight into the difference in thinking between men's and women's communities can be seen in the sometimes dramatic difference in programming in the communities and in the books offered for sale in the community bookshop. (It is not uncommon for the men's community, if Catholic, to offer very traditional conservative spiritual programming and traditional books often oriented to Mary, plus rosaries, statues, and so forth, while the women's community might be afire with the work of Thomas Berry, Teilhard de Chardin, Christian mystics, and eco-spirituality.)

The philosophy of this dynamic eco-spiritual leader, Albert Fritsch, reveals the source of his strength, the nature of his belief system:

> I hold the primacy of re-creative action involving appropriate technology to repair the environmental damage done to our Earth (resurrection-centered spirituality). I hold that a change of will and a change of the economic system of our world are of greater urgency than environmental education taken by itself. I hold that the poor and that women hold a key to this revolution through the inherent attributes that they have and express in their own way. I hold that the greatest and most important ecological problem facing religious communities is the passing on of their physical facilities and charisma to others without seeing these diminished or threatened by New Age concepts. I hold we begin in practical solving of concrete problems and this colors the philosophy which will follow—not what comes before. I believe that, for the Christian, Christ is to be the omega point and source of all we do and say, and that this must be explicitly stated in the course of a treatment of an eco-spirituality. And I believe in the importance of internal

prayerful discernment and external assessment of resources so that the healing process will begin.[24]

Al Fritsch clearly respects action, believing we live in a world of too much talk and too little action. He reflects that the nuns' groups were often influenced to do things because thinkers did not say or do enough, and that it is the activists who are the ones who articulate a Christian spirituality, not the "thinkers." All of this has been crucial to understanding Albert Fritsch's work, his Appalachian and national ministry, and to understand the critical foundational role he has played in Sisters of Earth and with the broader question of church lands and the role of church on the land. His recent report, *Reflections on Land Stewardship*[25] (March 2001), is a tangible summary of much of that work and thought.

The National Catholic Rural Life Conference (NCRLC) in Des Moines, Iowa, nationally organized but with much of its focus in the agricultural heartland of the Midwest and Great Plains, has taken serious interest in church lands and their usage, particularly with respect to assisting and alleviating rural community problems and insuring good land stewardship according to ecological principles and over the very long term.[26] Its ten-year project on church lands has also served to assist many of these same religious orders on the land, especially in giving them a sense of their common problems and challenges, and helping them to understand the breadth and scope of the national situation. Both the work of Albert Fritsch in this area and that of NCRLC have raised the stakes for the orders and for the Church as a whole. As this work and the spotlight it affixes on these lands has increased, the pressure on those with management and custodial responsibilities over these properties (lands and buildings) has demanded they walk their talk. By no means has this worked in all cases, but it is an increasing lever to bring about ecologically correct behavior or face the consequence of some direct embarrassment, maybe worse. Assisting this process around the country have been the increasing number of Catholic Bishops' pastoral letters on the environment, increasingly public statements which require in their wake more attention to "walking the talk." Thus, institutional structures can play the role of encouraging a disinterested or only mildly interested decision maker over the land and communities to make more progress in the ecological sustainability direction, perhaps developing some degree of higher motive, of spirituality, during the process. It is, however, the passionate and dedicated members of the Sisters of Earth, the monasteries, and others who are showing the way and clearing the path.

American Indian social activist Winona LaDuke, whose White Earth Land Recovery Project in Minnesota is a further example of sustainability on the land, has said, with respect to nuns and social activism: take them with you when you go to testify—they have so much moral conviction and determination that your cause will be a lot more effective.[27] That moral standing, conviction and determination is not missing from their eco-communities!

The statement issued at the close of Al Fritsch's Land Stewardship Conference for Religious Communities in summer 2000 could well encapsulate the message of this chapter. It reads:

> We claim kinship with the Earth community, a passionate concern for and spiritual connection with the land.
> The web of life is threatened. The land, air and water are at risk. We are suffering from: a loss of biodiversity, non-sustainable development, degradation of land, insufficient Earth knowledge, global atmospheric changes, loss of wilderness places to nurture our spirits and for wildlife habitats.
> We pledge to foster an ecological awareness that comes from a deep reverence and strong commitment to a right relationship with Earth.
> We support the voices of Earth which speak about a culture of life—biodiversity, communion and interdependence—in the sacred web of life.
> We commit ourselves to listen to the voices of the land where we live or which is under our care and to take action based on those voices."
>
> Issued at Milford, Ohio, May 2000[28]

These ecologically inspired religious communities operate under the philosophy, solidly Judaeo-Christian and not unlike the concept held by many primitive cultures, that we hold land in temporary and community trust; that the land does not belong to us in any absolute sense; that it is held by us in temporary trust; that its use is partly conditioned by the needs of the greater community; and that the land deserves to be left in a better state than when we found it. They see land, in the words of Al Fritsch, as suffering (i.e., all the well known harm that has and is being done to the natural system), as vulnerable. They see land as kin (i.e., as community).

They see land as temporary gift. They see land as tangible. And they see themselves as needing to be models of justice, eco-justice, which inherently includes human justice, justice to people, justice to the Creation.

These communities are demonstrating an economic practice for, as Wendell Berry has said, "Christianity must necessarily include an economic practice, a right way of using nature."[29]

In keeping with the second principle of ecology, nature as guide, nature as teacher, nature as source of revelation, and in keeping with the statement of U.S. Catholic Bishops that "In elaborating a natural moral law, we look to natural processes themselves for norms for human behavior,"[30] these land-based religious communities are demonstrating to the world the practical links between sustainable agriculture, sustainable community, and spiritual identity. In making this linkage, these communities are the very epitome of what this book is about.

The Sisters of Earth and monastic and social justice/eco-justice communities and projects described in this volume constitute not simply a demonstrated vision of what is, but rather a vision of what could be. This, in fact, is the real focal point for this book, under the assumption that our contemporary society is without vision. Focus on prime outstanding projects and their numerous elements and characteristics, as these are integrated into the charisms, the Christian and other religious social teaching, and other spiritual and religious principles, as they are integrated within faith belief, is what constitutes the essence of the meaning of this book. To keep a little humanity going in a sea of inhumanity is not bad work.

All of the women religious described herein would probably fit the American Lutheran theologian Larry Rasmussen's categorization of a people who don't live on Earth but who live in earth as earth.

Although the majority of Sisters of Earth communities are not constituted of monastic orders, some are. Additionally, there are monastic communities of a number of religious orders which have strong ecological values, and yet are not part of the evolution of the Sisters of Earth movement. Thus, monasticism deserves a separate treatment and stands on its own, as a particularly rich source of eco-spirituality in practice.

Chapter Six

MONASTICISM, SUSTAINABILITY, AND ECOLOGY

Amidst the forested hills of southern New Hampshire once lay Epiphany Monastery, home of a monastic community of New Camaldolese Benedictine monks. Their monastery, recently closed due to an insufficiency of monks, is a magnificently preserved eighteenth-century New England farmhouse with associated barns and outbuildings, placed on what was in that century one hundred acres of farm and pasture; now, it is fully grown to dense rather mature woodland of northern hardwoods and pine. Within this monastery house is a parlor and what we might call a "glassed in sunroom," always bright with the sun's rays and always open and inviting to an outdoors filled with chipmunks, red and gray squirrels, numerous songbirds, flowers, gardens, shrubs, and trees. In this sunroom, which in fact is the monastery's chapel, each day at 11:00 A.M. was celebrated, in the direct presence of the Creation, an ode to the Creator, the liturgy of the Mass. It was not unusual during the celebration of this liturgy to hear clear melodious birdsong coming in from the surrounding woodland. And it happens on occasion that the Mass was stopped midstream for periods, in order that all present might listen to the birdsong, to listen to and value the message of the Creator coming through the Creation. Interrupting a Mass in order to listen to birdsong, and to accept that birdsong as originating with the Creator, to treasure and reverence it as sacred, is not exactly common in Catholic or, indeed, in any Christian circles. And yet it goes far to illustrate the basic Christian theological concept of immanence, of God everywhere, of God in all, of the Creator in the Creation, and therefore of the sacrality of all. Here is the essence of eco-spirituality, of creation spirituality, the essence of the theology of ecology, the theology of Creation. And it was being practiced by a twelve-centuries old order of Catholic monks in the woodlands of New Hampshire. To say that what is commonly thought of as mainstream Catholicism, mainstream Christianity, as Western religion or as the Church in the West has become far removed from this would be a big understatement. That, perhaps, suggests the magnitude of the problem, and the magnitude of hope we may hold for the future. It also suggests the potential for the Christian monastic communities in our midst. As many people today feel the need to affirm simplicity, stewardship, harmony, and stability, a reexamination of monasticism is pertinent.

What is the message of the man in the desert from whom monasticism arose?

BACKGROUND

Christianity's book of revelation, the Bible, gives us the image of John the Baptist alone and suffering and becoming strengthened in the desert, a synonym for remoteness, for isolation, for being alone, and particularly for being alone with oneself, of finding oneself in the aloneness, the solitude. The Bible also gives us this image, this message, with Christ himself, for forty days and forty nights.

But it was a few centuries later, when confusion arose concerning the core meanings of Christianity, of Christ's teaching, and when distance, distortion, and corruption of that teaching, all inevitable, had set in human society, that a new lesson could be learned. For it was at this time that a young Anthony of Egypt, a teenager who had settled his affairs in the world and discharged his responsibilities, took leave of the world for a lengthy period of perhaps twenty-five years, and entered the desert region of Egypt east of the Nile to be fully alone, to live the life of a hermit with no human contact. After these many years, he again reemerged and rejoined human society, to live many more years amongst humanity. A philosopher asked St. Anthony: "Father, how can you be enthusiastic when the comfort of books has been taken away from you?" He replied: "My book, O philosopher, is the nature of created things, and whenever I want to read the word of God, it is usually right in front of me."[1] It is from Anthony, and with the great assistance of his contemporary and biographer, Athanasius, that all Christian monks and the very idea of Christian monasticism and the contemplative life, takes its inspiration. We might well ask ourselves what can we learn of reality and the ecologic concept from this monastic or contemplative experience. A reexamination of monasticism is pertinent, as many people today feel the need to affirm simplicity, stewardship, harmony, and stability.

Christian monasticism merges with the subject of ecological thought and sustainable living on three levels:

1. For more than sixteen centuries, Christian monasticism has offered Western civilization a model of stewardship and sustainability;

2. Christian monasticism in particular and the contemplative life in general offer a way of entry, as it were, or a rite of passage to a deeper more reflective and simpler, ecologically conducive lifestyle which holds the promise of great insight into reality and into true ecological thought;

3. Christian monasticism is thoroughly countercultural to modern society, in a world in need of working models of counterculturalism, a world in need of models to deeply challenge the status quo, where the culture of consumption is the conventional wisdom.

Monasticism in the West developed and grew partly in response to the loss of the stability of the secular society with the decline and fall of the Roman Empire and the chaos and turmoil which resulted. Monasticism in Christian tradition also grew in response to the distortion of the message of Christ and the associated corruption of the Christian church within just a few centuries of Christ's lifetime. In the first context, it was an escape and a search for stability in an increasingly unstable world. In the latter, it was a reform movement, perhaps the very first of many subsequent attempts at reforming Christianity.

People who know of Western monasticism think of it in the context of Saint Benedict of Nursia, his life and the development of his Rule (the Rule of Benedict), and the subsequent emergence in Italy of what was to become the Benedictine Order, an Order which survives worldwide to this day. But the "father" of all monks is not Benedict but rather an Egyptian, Anthony of Egypt, who lived a few hundred years prior to Benedict.

Benedict and his monks, the Benedictines, were most closely associated with the concept of escaping from the turmoil of the secular world by seeking shelter in monasteries and their monastic communities which were, in a sense, the "new towns" of their day. Anthony is associated with a protest against a young but already too worldly and corrupt religious institution, the Roman Christian church of the year A.D. 200. At the same time, he experimented with an alternative lifestyle which held promise of a more direct communication with God and deeper insight into the meaning of nature and reality.

A search for an answer to the deeper questions of ecological thought might well start with the remarkable story of Anthony of Egypt, the founding model of monasticism and the first monk in the West. In order to establish the context for the modern reader, one must first consider the reality of life on Earth from the earliest up until comparatively recent times, the preelectricity, preindustrial world, and a world of far fewer human beings relative to space and land and the vastness of the planet. This is a world that even our forebears of a mere century ago could much more readily understand than can we in the so-called modern or postmodern era. Such was a world of majesty, wonder, awe, fear, magic, and of what we now call "superstition," a world in which we humans had far lesser grounds to give in to the sin of pride, hubris, arrogance, a world in which it was easy to feel small and inferior, not superior as at present. We neither managed nor manipulated on a grand scale for we could not. We had a proper sense of the mystical in a way that we pretend not to have in more modern times. It is important, therefore, to understand not only that many basic human attitudes were different in Anthony's time, but also that those attitudes, those frameworks for organizing knowledge, those ways of knowing, were prevalent among humanity for long years prior to Anthony and typify many centuries through the premedieval, medieval and postmedieval eras down to at least the last century. They are the attitudes and the ways of knowing which have formed us. These ways are undoubtedly still with us today but repressed, making us feel much more distant from nature, from life, from death, from the spirit. We thereby find it much more difficult to cultivate a sense of awe, of reverence, and thus easily give in to the temptation to distance ourselves more from reality, and to thereby gain the means to destroy our immediate context (the life systems of the planet) and thus ourselves in the process. Anthony, who lived so many centuries ago, had a more realistic attitude toward the nature of reality and the necessary attitudes required by life.

In comparison to the present, we may view the world of Anthony and most of the centuries since as more mystical and awe-inspiring in their nature. It is a world we may be too quick to judge and to discount as superstitious and yet we must not yield to that temptation if we are to gain insight from Anthony's remarkable story.

Al Fritsch, environmental scientist, ecological ethicist, Jesuit priest, sustainability practitioner par excellence, and one who is not a monastic, has written:

> The image that is good to use with reference to a monastery in this age of environmental crisis is a place of stability, a sure point of reference, where residents are living testimony to the harmony of prayer and work. People often do not reflect on the mystery of Creation and they do not pace their work or activity habits in a human manner. What the monastery does is to present a model for all to follow in a relaxed but meaningful manner. This way of acting and being is in tune with the place and ecosystem and serves as a model of what the world should become in its more perfect future. The monastery is not an escape from the "world" but a premier location for good ecological practice required to re-create a better world."[2]

MONASTICISM AND SUSTAINABILITY

For those who might wonder if a monastery can offer a strong model of sustainability, I posit the following personal experience; a brush with real sustainability.

Have you ever wondered what real sustainability would be like? Would you know it if you saw it? My wife and I had a brush with real sustainability, or at least we think we did, out on the American prairie.

Upon entering one monastery's refectory (dining commons), we couldn't help but notice the heavy wooden tables and chairs. We sensed there was something a little bit different about them. It wasn't long, however, before we took them for granted. But there WAS something a little bit different. Gradually, after a few visits, we began to see things in greater detail. The chairs were certainly heavy but slid over the floor with ease and no damage.

Most New Englanders are familiar with the plain and simple yet elegant and graceful lines of Shaker furniture. Shaker furniture this was not. And New England this was not. We were at the forest/prairie edge in western Minnesota. We were at a monastery, a Benedictine women's and nearby men's community of monks.

Continuing to wonder about these tables and chairs that had caught our attention, by the third day we asked about how old they were. About one hundred years old, we were told. And in perfect condition! These tables and chairs which we and the whole community were using every day were a century old and represented a design and manner of production over a century old—that's what made us sense there was something different about them.

One hundred year old institutional tables and chairs, in continuous and heavy use for all meals for all of that time! (That's 109,500 meals served at each place setting, plus all other events and usages.) Now that's sustainability!

We then asked how and where they were made. And where did the wood come from? We learned that they were made from the monastery's own woodland, one hundred years ago. And that may suggest that in-house design and manufacture was more feasible then than today, given the greater proliferation of cottage industry a century ago. And it might even be argued that wood from one's own woodland and sawmill were somewhat more likely a century back, given the small nature of towns, open space, cheap land, and peoples' general closeness to Nature.

But if you were to ask the question, How are these chairs repaired today, or, when needed, replaced, the answer would be the very same: repaired, rebuilt, replaced from their own woodshop and from their own wood from their own woodland. Even today!

And what about that woodland? We walked to it (yes, it's that close), and found an uneven-aged stand of hardwood (deciduous) forest composed of several species of oaks, maples, basswood, birch, ironwood, and other hardwoods, with a few pine. About 10 percent was old growth. Harvesting was conducted with horses for most of its history (and still partially today), cutting was very selective and governed by specific needs, and overall yield was on a 90–100 year rotation. If these things don't point to quality in both management of the resource and in the finished product it yields, I don't know what does!

Returning indoors to the presence of these graceful and elegant tables and chairs, now a century old, and returning to them not once but three times a day, we were invited to learn something else. Would we like to know the individuals who actually built these one hundred years ago? A short walk out the refectory and down a path led to the marked graves of the now long dead monks (sisters) who built this furniture. The monastery records are detailed and clear in relating such information, and the graves are easily found.

We felt the circle had been completed.

This experience clearly describes a brush with sustainability, ecological, and otherwise. We have a new (or very old) model for our ecological, environmental, and sustainability studies.

SECULAR APPROACHES TO MONASTICISM

Two important secular voices not associated with monasticism or Christianity have spoken out in recent years about the monastic way as a model for sustainability: Theodore Roszak, social and environmental historian, and Morris Berman, social historian and culture critic.

In his 1979 book, *Person/Planet*,[3] environmental historian Theodore Roszak wrote extensively of Christian monasticism as sustainability model, hearkening back to the nearly two thousand year history of the monastic form in his chapter "Monastic Economics" (and as also quoted in a 1981 issue of *Benedictines*). In a letter to Roszak, Trappist monk Matthew Kelty wrote: "If anything is needed in this hour it is men (*sic*) who know their way around in the desert, men who can understand what is going on there, can interpret it, manage with it. To be a monk in this time, then, is really to be the man of the hour. . . . The desert is the monk's world and today the world is a desert."[4] (The irony of this non-inclusive language is that women, too, are monastics and, in fact, any monk or nun with an interest in this area, male or female, would admit that the leadership at the conflation of monasticism and ecology is coming from women.) The original monasteries of the Western world were, according to Roszak, an imaginative and popular response to the long-term social crisis of their times. According to Roszak: "The achievements of that movement—its durability as an anarchist economic form, its wise eye for the spiritual needs of the person—are everything that the leadership of our very secular, very practical world forgets or ignores when it begins casting about for realistic lines of policy."[5] He argues we must learn from that sense of mutual aid and self-reliance, that appreciation of the wealth inherent in simplicity that characterizes monastic life. Roszak writes:

> My interest is in monasticism as a model, a tested historical paradigm of creative social disintegration. I turn to it because it illuminates the way in which the top-heavy and toxic institutions of an exhausted empire were sifted down into civilized, durable communities where a vital new sense of human identity and destiny could take root."[6]

Referring to the monastic way as one which balances technical innovation and ecological intelligence, Roszak provides the historical evidence as to why the monastic model might be of value to us in our time for ". . . their relations with the land remained frugal and gentle; their technology was always kept to a moderate scale. . . . (T)he monasteries never regarded economic activity as an end in itself, never idolized productivity, never measured their success by profit or by any criterion of competitive national power. . . . (T)heir economics sprang from a work ethic that regarded manual labor as a spiritual discipline. 'Ora et labora'—and one worked as one prayed, in the pursuit of personal sanctification."[7] None other than Lewis Mumford found, according to Roszak, that the monks had found the secret of true leisure, ". . . not as freedom from work . . . but as freedom within work; and, along with that, time to converse, to ruminate, to contemplate the meaning of life."[8]

Fundamental from an ecological perspective, he argues that monasteries have developed an economic order that respects the rights of the planet and "they achieve a wise and harmonious rapport with the Earth."[9]

We hear much today about voluntary simplicity which, among other things, including human scale and ecological awareness, Roszak defines as a style of life which is nonconsumptive and which focuses upon being and becoming, not on having. This is almost exactly the economic style of the monastic paradigm.

Roszak asks us to "Imagine that it (the monastery) might become the social framework for honorable small businesses, for labor—barter co-ops, for craft and professional collectives, for community development cooperatives, for worker-controlled shops and plants, and . . . it might assimilate the most ingeniously appropriate forms of modern technology. Even if there must occasionally be robes, bells, and mantras in the picture, think of them surrounded by solar collectors, . . . methane digesters, the full repertory of people's technology which seeks to dignify and facilitate the work of human hands, not to eliminate it as a curse."[10]

Reflecting on what came about so many centuries ago, Roszak says of the monasteries

> . . . their impact on our future, on the tastes and values of our society, will never be adequately gauged by a mere nose-counting sociology. Nor can they expect their efforts to be acknowledged or encouraged in the cultural mainstream, any more than we could have expected even the keenest political minds of dying Rome to recognize in their day that the next chapter in Western history would be written by the scruffy and uncivil likes of a St. Anthony (the first Christian monk) ruminating in the wilderness, working, praying, building a new society out of sweat and rubble beyond the horizons of their age.[11]

In Roszak's view, monasteries are clearly worth our attention.

Another contemporary social historian with no personal connection to monasteries has seen fit to focus his recent book *The Twilight of American Culture* on the very idea of monasticism as a response to the American crisis. In Morris Berman's early chapter, "The Monastic Option," he relates the story of the well-known role of the monasteries in preserving stability in a sea of chaos, in preserving the culture of learning through a dark period that threatened to destroy it, and in elevating the importance and role of contemplation in human life. Then, in his chapter "The Monastic Option in the Twenty-first Century," Berman shares his belief that the only survival through the chaos and destruction of contemporary culture death will be through a new class of individual, not physically located in any one place, monastery or otherwise, but people engaged in a practice and way of life very much counter to the mainstream culture, independent people who think for themselves and resist the mass culture. He describes the new monastic individual (or "NMI") as

> the class of people that belong to no class, have no membership in a hierarchy. They form a kind of "unnamed aristocracy," free of bosses, supervision, and what is typically called "work." They work very hard, in fact, but as they love their work and do it for its intrinsic interest, this work is

not much different from play. . . . (S)uch people are an anomaly, for they have no interest in the world of business success and mass consumerism.[12]

Berman further gives examples of what might constitute the monastic option:

> traditions of craftsmanship, care and integrity; preservation of canons of scholarship, critical thinking, and the Enlightenment tradition; combating the forces of environmental degradation and social inequality; valuing individual achievement and independent thought. . . . But central to all of these examples is the rejection of a life based on kitsch, consumerism, and profit, or on power, fame, and self-promotion.[13]

Monasticism stands as a critique of the mainstream culture, for there is much about it which is countercultural. Hence, there is a value in understanding what monasticism has to say to ecology and sustainability. There is also a value in knowing what well-regarded secular social critics and historians like Theodore Roszak and Morris Berman have to say about monasticism's possible influence over how we are to deal with our ecological sustainability challenges.

Another secular lay person writing extensively on monasticism and modern life, and with a strong sense of place and ecological concern, is poet and essayist Kathleen Norris, undoubtedly the most popular American writer on this subject. Norris presents an astute observance of the monastic lifestyle and how it might contrast with and provide a new model for a more ecological and much more meaningful lifestyle. Norris deals in her writings with the liturgical sense of time, with *ora et labora* (prayer and work), with the psalms, with ceremony, with earth and soul in relationship, and with consumption.

Norris finds that the greatest difference between monastic life and any other life is the liturgical sense of time. She and many others have often reflected that upon first entry into a monastery, time seems to stand still. The ability of monastics to maintain a schedule centered on the liturgy sets them apart from the rest of us and, over the years, submission to liturgical time yields the development of a playful patience that, she finds, is very much at odds with worldly values.

The Benedictine motto, "*ora et labora*," insists, Norris believes, that work is prayer, as long as we maintain a playful attitude toward that work and offer it as prayer. Moderation, too, is essential, for lack of proportion always corrupts, and what sets monks apart from the rest of us is not an overbearing piety, perhaps something the lay person might expect, but rather a contemplative sense of fun.

Martin Buber, the Jewish theologian, has written that means, that is, the very way in which we do things, the way we make the journey, might constitute our life's work. Norris writes that the Benedictines are a good illustration of Buber's point:

> Although their members follow a common way of life, monasteries do not produce cookie cutter monks and nuns. Just the opposite. Monasteries have a unity that is remarkably unrestrained by uniformity; they are comprised of distinct individuals, often memorable characters, whose eccentricities live for generations in the community's oral history.[14]

Norris sees the monastery as akin to the chemistry lab and wonders if religion might be seen as an experiment in human chemistry.

One might well wonder about a connection between psalms of the Jewish heritage, so central to the life of monasteries, and ecological sustainability. Kathleen Norris has no hesitancy to make the connection for us. She writes that the monks' dependence upon and deep involvement with the psalms changes them, makes them different, even separates them from the American culture. She describes psalms as disruptive, hard to take, and mostly centered outside of Christian worship in America. In the psalms there is a constant movement between the mundane and the exalted. God behaves in the psalms, Norris writes, in ways he is not allowed to behave in Christian theology. Rough-hewn from earthly experience, the psalms, she says, are absolutely different from formal prayer. Norris presents the monastic community as something different from the mainstream when she writes: ". . . (A)s Benedictine prayer roles on, as daily as marriage and washing dishes, it tends to sweep away the concerns of systematic theology and Church doctrine."[15]

Norris describes three paradoxes in the psalms: (1) within them, pain is missed in praise (which I take to mean being overcome by praise); (2) while the psalms speak most directly to the individual, they cannot be removed from a communal context; and (3) the psalms are holistic in insisting that the mundane and the holy are inextricably linked. The last is a particularly valuable insight for this volume but all serve to help identify and differentiate the countercultural lifestyle of the monastery. Norris finds, with respect to the psalms, that

- the monastic method of reading the psalms, with long silences between them rather than with commentary or explanation, highlights and strengthens the paradoxes, offering, she says, almost alarming room for interpretation and response;

- the world the psalms depict is not so different from our own;

- the psalms become like a mirror to the person singing them;

- the psalms have a strong social justice and, by derivation, an eco-justice component in that they remind us it is the powerless in society who are overwhelmed when injustice becomes institutionalized—not comfortable reading, Norris says, and very much against the American grain;

- whereas the true religions of America are optimism and denial, the psalms demand that we recognize that praise does not spring from a delusion that things are better than they are, but rather for the human capacity for joy;

- the psalms are as a heartbeat to monks, they become a part of a monk's physical as well as spiritual life, acting on the heart to slow it down;

- the psalms mirror our world but do not allow us to become voyeurs; they force us to recognize our own part in our violence, including violence against nature; they make us reexamine our values; they let us know the depths of the damage we do when we enslave other people, when we blithely consume the cheap products of cheap labor—they ask us to be honest about ourselves;

- the psalms can heighten our sense of marvel and awaken our capacity to appreciate the glories of this world, a fundamentally necessary position if one is to behave ecologically.

Reenforcing such views on the psalms and their central place in monasticism is the monastic tradition of *Lectio Divina* (divine reading), which has three major interpenetrating steps: *lectio, meditatio,* and *comtemplatio* (reading, meditation, and comtemplation). The first one is a movement of the reader who performs the act of reading; the second is the act of the book that "reads" the reader; the third is a unifying process, where reader and book become one. The psalms and monasticism thus give us an otherworldly and highly alternative view to modern life, one which opens approaches to sustainability and spirituality which might otherwise be unavailable.

Norris gives a high priority to good ceremony, to liturgy, in that it allows for all the dimensions of human experience, and thus the possibility of transformation. She contends that ceremony requires that we work with others in the humbling give and take of communal existence and that it forces a person to slow down. Thus, encountering monastic prayer or a traditional monastic meal eaten in silence to the accompaniment of a reader can feel like skidding to a halt.

Monasticism also teaches us to be wary of definitions, since they put boundaries that impose limits, in contrast to proceeding by paradox and symbol, the preferred monastic way. Norris reminds us that early Christianity did not accept a dichotomy between earth and soul, an important characteristic of the foundations of monasticism.

Norris and many other writers on monasticism hold that the psalms teach that "Greed is at the heart of the story, greed expressed in sexual terms, which translates into rape. Consumerism is our idolatry, the heart of our illusions of power, security and self-sufficiency, which translate into rape of the environment."[16] Thomas Berry, Passionist monk, refers to psalms as the cosmic liturgy, the interspersion of the human experience into the cosmological.[17]

Given the above from secular writers on monasticism, we might look at what monastics themselves have had to say on monasticism and sustainability.

MONKS ON MONASTICISM

Thomas Merton, Trappist monk of Kentucky, is by far the most well-known monastic writer in the United States. Merton had much to contribute to modern day linkages between monasticism and ecology, and to contemporary eco-spirituality, even though he died in 1968, before ecological thinking entered the mainstream. Since his writings are so voluminous, widespread and available, I will refrain from an overindulgence on Merton here, except for a limited attention to lesser known Merton thoughts. In his book, *The Wisdom of the Desert*, Merton recognized the gap between the secular culture, ancient or modern, when he wrote of the earliest monastics, the "desert fathers," as they were called (there were also desert mothers, albeit lesser known): "These were men who believed that to let oneself drift along, passively accepting the tenets and values of what they knew as society, was purely and simply a disaster. The fact that the Emperor (of Rome) was now Christian and that the "world" was coming to know the Cross as a sign of temporal power only strengthened them in their resolve" (to reject mainstream culture).[18] An important ecological contribution of Merton's to the monastic dialogue was his strong link to the religions and philosophies of the East, to Buddhism and Hinduism, and particularly to Zen. This came from his recognition that the "Desert Fathers" had much in common with Indian Yogis and with Zen Buddhist monks of China and Japan. If we were to seek their like in twentieth-century America "we would have to look in strange out of the way places."[19] In his book *Mystics and Zen Masters*, Merton writes of Zen as the ontological awareness of pure being beyond subject and object, an immediate grasp of being in its "suchness" and "thusness." He says Zen insight is not our awareness, but Being's awareness of itself in us. "The whole world is aware of itself in me,"[20] a precise evocation of another monk, Thomas Berry, who developed these ideas decades later and is centrally important to this study. Merton continues: "I am no longer my individual and limited self, but my 'identity' is to be sought not in that separation from all that is, but in oneness, in convergence with all that is. . . . This identity is not the denial of my own personal identity but its highest affirmation. It is a discovery of genuine identity in and with the One."[21] And in *The Wisdom of the Desert*, Merton concludes with respect to those early monks and monastic founders: "The simple men who lived their lives out to a good old age among the rocks and sands only did so because they had come into the desert to be themselves, their ordinary selves, and to forget a world that divided them from themselves."[22] The connectedness of Thomas Merton, monasticism, Thomas Berry, Eastern philosophy, and early Christianity with ecological thought and environmental sustainability is undeniable, if not well known. And Fr. Romuald, a contemporary monk in California, echoes this thinking precisely when he says: "If you're going to be like Anthony (the first monk), you have to be in union with all creation—you can never get redeemed in isolation—that's impossible in Christianity—one is redeemed in the cosmos by the cosmic Christ"[23]—a Christian statement, obviously, but could any statement be more ecological?

Powerful ecological thoughts come also from the pen of Br. Benet Tvedten, O.S.B., also a contemporary Benedictine monk. With respect to the Rule of Benedict, the sixteen hundred year old rule book for Benedictine monks, men and women, worldwide (and the most common form of Christian monasticism), Br. Benet states: "The Rule indicates what St. Benedict disliked: grumbling, laziness, wastefulness, indifference, arrogance. And what he liked: a sense of responsibility, honesty, temperance, simplicity. He gave us a regulated life. He had us profess a vow of stability."[24] It is that vow of stability which marks the monastic life as unusual and also gives it a very strong sense of place, a critical ecological value. On the subject of consumption, also critical to ecology, Br. Benet quotes Benedict: "Whoever needs less should thank God and not be distressed, but whoever needs more should feel humble because of his weakness, not self-important because of the kindness shown him"[25]—indeed, a very strong anticonsumption and proecological sentiment. And Benet shares another important Benedictine belief: "The monastery should, if possible, be so constructed that within it all necessities, such as water, mill and garden are contained, and the various crafts practiced. There will be no need for the monks to roam outside . . .",[26] a reenforcement of sense of place, and of sustainable living par excellence. One might also, however, see in this a discounting of the notion of interdependence, perhaps a weakness of Benedictine monasticism.

Terrence Kardong, O.S.B., is regarded as one of the foremost writers today on monasticism and the land, monasticism and ecology. Writing in *Embracing Earth: Catholic Approaches to Ecology*, Kardong concludes that the value of the Rule of Benedict to ecology and sustainability are not to be found in a search for precise words in the Rule which promote ecological values but rather on the centrality within that Rule and concomitant way of life of humility, stability, and frugality. Since humility, according to Kardong, is the central virtue promoted by the Rule, and is central as well to avoidance of the human arrogance and hubris which is so detrimental to the planet and its ecosystems, to the Creation if you will, the guiding rule of modern day Christian monasticism comes through as strongly ecological in a most basic way. (One must also bear in mind here that "humility" comes from "humus," which means soil.) Kardong also takes the command to be humble as extending to all creatures, not just humans. "If humility is to be given full expression . . . the human person must not only be humble before God but also before the merest living member of God's creation.[27]

The unusual vow of stability is one of three vows a Benedictine must take. This does not mean that monks do not travel; the issue is relative and proportional. It does mean, however, ". . . that some degree of physical stability is of vital importance in shaping human attitudes toward the earth."[28] It is known that those who are stable in a place have the biggest stake in it. This leads to ". . . the ecological truism that degradation of our environment inevitably leads to degradation of our-selves."[29] Terrence Kardong would find himself in full agreement with the important American environmental philosopher Wendell Berry when Kardong writes: "To really get to know and love a place, a person must live there and live there for a long time. . . . (T)hose who live in a place are usually in the best position to know what is appropriate for that place . . ."[30]

The concept of frugality is also a central tenet of Benedictine monasticism. There is strong caution against any confusion between wants and needs, wants being recognized as insatiable unless held in check. Much, of course, could be written about the relationship between frugality and ecology, for ecological principle demands frugality, balance, lack of excess. Kardong in his writings reminds us that also coming out of the monastic aspect of frugality is the very important ecological dictate that a person live on what is locally available, directly akin to both the Christian principle of subsidiarity and the Buddhist teachings in the "Eight-fold Noble Path to Right Livelihood," that we restrict ourselves as much as possible in fulfillment of our physical needs to those local sources over which we can accept moral responsibility and accountabil-ity. Supporting local farmers and independently owned local business for the fulfillment of all or most of our physical needs derives directly from this idea. Frugality, simplicity, monasticism all fit perfectly together, for monasticism requires both frugality and simplicity.

Terrence Kardong is also much known for his writings on monasti-cism, the land, and agriculture. In his essay, "Monks and the Land," Kar-dong supports stability, for example, "To work where you live means to understand where you are, and what you are doing. Home territory is by definition turf that one knows intimately."[31] He says: "Real farming is an art that can only be learned in community. It takes generations to accu-mulate wisdom about the proper way to farm a given district. This is a different sort of knowledge from that learned at the agricultural college. The communal question is not just how I can turn the biggest profit, but how I can leave the land better than I found it for my successors. . . . The Rule of Benedict assumes a wisdom context where age and experience are more highly valued than abstract analytic data."[32]

Fr. Hugh Feiss, O.S.B., monk of the desert wilderness of the Pacific Northwest, takes us down an ecological and yet slightly different path. In his essay, "Watch the Crows: Environmental Responsibility and the Bene-dictine Tradition," Feiss not only writes extensively of humility and stability, but also adds attention to universal reverence, not only for God or human life, but also for tools (which must, according to the Rule of Benedict, also be treated as sacred as the utensils of the altar) and, as well, reverence for physical things (nature). In commenting on the idea that the Rule requires that monks wear clothing available from the local vicinity, Feiss calls this ". . . a far cry from golf courses in the desert, strawberries in December, and grocery stores where the average product is transported over 1,300 miles before reaching the shelves of the store!"[33] This places monks squarely on the ecological and countercultural side of modern life, at least when they are living to their ideals. Along these lines, "Benedict's monk would certainly be out of place in a culture whose measures of success are power and money, which employs maximum technological force to squeeze as much as possible out of the natural world as quickly as possible.[34] He continues: "Benedict's monks are told to live in a way that will make them friends of the planet and not its enemies."[35] And Feiss goes on to explain that his own point is ". . . not to glorify Benedictines unduly but to find in their rich tradition guidance for human beings who want to live as part of the seamless garment of nature."[36] Fr. Hugh Feiss is an active part of the monastic ecological story of which he writes.

In any survey of monasticism and ecology, one could also cite the work of Trappist monk Fr. Charles Cummings of Utah, Carmelites William McNamara and Tessa Bielecki of Colorado, and Passionist Gail Worcelo of Vermont (of whom more later), contemporary monks all, who have contributed passionately to the dialogue. No contemporary monastic writer is better or more widely known today, however, than the scholar of Benedictine monasticism, Sr. Joan Chittister, O.S.B. Sr. Joan in her many books stresses the Benedictine commitment to conversion and is a foremost national spokesperson for the nature of Benedictine spirituality, which she refers to in the very ecological way, a spirituality of cosmic connectedness, connectedness of time, land, people, things, all as vehicles of the Holy. Benedictine spirituality forcefully argues that we cannot make ourselves our only life agenda, that "we must live life for something greater than (our) satisfactions and . . . not let anything or anyone cause (us) to lose hold on (our) free and unfettered self."[37] She identifies as tools of the spiritual craft silence, custom, the common table, *statio, lectio,* manual labor, and stewardship. "Monastic spirituality says we must learn to listen to the cacaphony within us in order to defy its demands and to dampen its hold on us."[38] With respect to silence, "Life without silent space is not life at all . . . (W)ithout some semblance of silence every day, there can be no such thing as monastic spirituality at all."[39] With respect to the common table, "In Benedictine spirituality, eating is not an act of survival. Eating is an act of community."[40] "*Statio*" is defined as "the practice of stopping one thing before we begin another."[41] "*Statio*" is meant to center us and make us more conscious of what we're doing. "'*Statio*' is the virtue of presence,"[42] according to Chittister. "*Lectio*" refers to sacred reading, which does not set out to teach but rather to enlighten. "*Lectio*" is ". . . the monastic practice designed to remind us always of who we are and what we have yet to grow into in this particular moment in life."[43]

Stewardship calls us to do as well as to be, to act, to preserve, to physically care for, to make things including land last. "Benedictine spirituality . . . simply does not believe in indiscriminate consumption,"[44] says Joan Chittister. And manual labor, an active commitment to the stewardship of the Earth, work with our hands, is action that makes everyone equal. It is humility in practice.

Thus, Benedictine monastic spirituality ". . . is manifested in a distinctive attitude of life that values silence and custom and '*statio*' and '*lectio*' and stewardship and manual labor and the common table. All of them speak of the holiness of life. All of them develop insight in us rather than learning. All of them plunge us into life rather than take us out of it. All of them require us to look and look again at things until we see them right,"[45] very much opposite to the commonly held popular view of monasticism, and all of them strongly supportive of ecological viewpoints and practice. Chittister concludes: "The function of Benedictine spirituality . . . is simply the cultivation of monastic mindfulness,"[46] fully in keeping with Buddhist monasticism and Eastern philosophy, and virtually necessary for eco-spirituality and sustainability.

There is some interrelationship between Benedictine spirituality and American Indian thought and tradition. This link comes in part from the fact that there are many Benedictine monasteries in Indian country. The American Indian philosopher Vine DeLoria's perspectives on Native Americans' environmental and spiritual values conjoins well with the Benedictine spirit of humility, their stance of openness and compassion, their acknowledgement that we can learn from others.[47] Professor Russell Butkus of the University of Portland, a scholar of monasticism, advocates a definition of sustainability put forth by theologian Larry Rasmussen as ". . . the capacity of natural and social systems to survive and thrive together indefinitely. It is also a vision with an implicit earth ethic. Both sustainability and its earth ethic follow from creation's integrity and a picture of earth as '*oikos*'."[48] Given this definition, Butkus believes ". . . the Benedictine tradition holds rich possibilities for incorporating the language and praxis of sustainability. . . . Benedictine monastic communities can become sacramental models of . . . sustainable communities."[49] Butkus also writes:

> Given the high degree of mobility in our culture, Benedict's teaching on stability of place would most likely be perceived as a countercultural (but necessary) palliative to our predicament of unsustainability but not nearly as countercultural, or as difficult to achieve, as the Benedictine virtue of frugality. This strikes at the very core of our unsustainable way of life. . . . The countercultural and perhaps subversive virtue of frugality is one of the most significant contributions the Benedictine tradition can make in our affluent society . . .[50]

In his paper "Indigenous Realization of Community: Clay Work and Worship, Shared Sensibility as a Common Rural Background of Benedictine Environment," Professor Richard Bresnahan of the Benedictine St. John's University links Benedictine spirituality directly to the seventeen principles of sustainability put forth by the distinguished American environmental philosopher Wendell Berry: "In many ways these seventeen benchmarks in sustainable action are similar to a contemporary clarification of the Rule of St. Benedict in the care of community within and without the monastic walls."[51] And, in linkage to American Indian spirituality: "Benedictines, rooted in the indigenous path of nature, can embrace and evolve patterns of lived spiritual experiences with nature and again be a model for this culture."[52]

None other than Fr. John Klassen, O.S.B., the monk who now serves as Abbott of the largest monastery in the United States, as well as a professor at St. John's University, links Benedictine monastic spirituality to the thought of one of the ecologically purest and most ecocentric writers in America, the environmental poet and practicing Buddhist Gary Snyder. He argues for the vow of stability as an excellent foundation for environmental stewardship and, as well, for the Earth's ability to serve as teacher and guide: "The earth can also teach us about our lives. All too often we think of other humans as our primary teachers. But earth can teach us about change in a unique way because it has a four billion year resume in the field."[53] Citing Gary Snyder's *The Practice of the Wild* and Snyder's belief that it's not enough to love nature or want to be in harmony with it—we must KNOW the flora and fauna, the natural systems, the complex web of relationships—Klassen writes: "It is precisely monastic stability which unites the spiritual journey with a profound commitment to environmental stewardship."[54] Responding to Snyder's call to honor this land's great antiquity, its wildness, and its role as our spiritual as well as our physical home, Klassen continues: "As Benedictine monastics we are precisely people who 'stay in a place long enough that the spirits can influence us'."[55] Such unity between an important Benedictine abbot and scholar and the ecological thought of Gary Snyder (and Annie Dillard, Wendell Berry, and other leading American ecocentric thinkers) yields insight into the nature of Benedictine monasticism in America today.

There is, of course, another side to this coin. Not all models of Benedictine spirituality are so ecologically sensitive, as a visitation to a cross section of the monasteries around the country would reveal a much more mixed picture. It has been said by some critics that Benedictines, in spite of their sixteen hundred year old vows, have been evangelized by the counterecological modern culture instead of evangelizing the culture, that Benedictines, to some extent, have lost a sense of their own charism. (The same could be said for the broader Catholic Church and for Christianity as a whole.) This being the case, there are Benedictine and other monasteries which appear to have no ecological values, or which, indeed, may even hold to antiecological values, a testament to their subversion by the culture in which they, as human beings and as a human institution, find themselves. Sustainability is a conversion experience, says Abbot Klassen. It is not simply a matter of tinkering. You either resist and oppose the mainstream culture or you yield to it and become part of it. There is no middle way. Monasticism appears to require cessation of the way in which we live, in terms of energy and ecology, in terms of place and the land.

WEAKNESSES OF MONASTICISM

Challenges to monasteries which often make it difficult to live ecologically include:

1. inheritance of large, old, energy wasteful buildings, which can't be put to much use, and which cannot be renovated without great monetary expenditure;

2. lay farmers and ranchers who have often been with the monastery for a very long time, are respected, and often are very conventional and noninnovative land managers who are not open to change;

3. lack of monks strongly interested in making changes, even if they are intellectually open-minded;

4. significant passivity and nonactivism of many monks; monks who are not necessarily opposed to activism and who could be led, but who will not initiate themselves;

5. strong ingrained philosophy in monastic organization of respecting peoples' running their own areas of work without interference—a structural guarantee of little or very slow change;

6. the aloneness of individuals who are activist and who can and will lead, but who are not supported by their community;

7. antiactivist and often antiecological pressure of the local surrounding culture in the rural agricultural area in which most monasteries are located;

8. some feeling against, or disinterest in, long-term planning or any planning;

9. economic concerns that lead to a "can't do" attitude no matter how meritorious or important the project.

These challenges are somewhat countered by the strong frugality ethic of many communities and the stability and sense of place which encourages a very long-term conservation ethic, not necessarily in service to an ethic of ecological sustainability but rather representing the community's interpretation of the requirements of the Rule of Benedict.

Balancing this, however, is the challenge to contemporary monks and monastic communities to answer these questions of their guiding rule:

*   Does the Rule of Benedict permit complicity with the forces of destruction, of soil, of water, of ecosystems, of human beings, of farmers, of farm and rural communities, of human and planetary health and balance, which are inherent in the cheap food,

chemically dependent and energy wasteful industrial agriculture, which is the source of most food sold in the United States, including that sold to many monasteries?

- Does the Rule of Benedict permit stealing from future generations yet unborn, a theft which is now explicitly prohibited in the new Catechism (rule) of their Church?

- Or, does the Rule of Benedict require that these communities which call themselves Benedictine, follow a different path, a path which includes serious effort at some food self-sufficiency, and a path which supports and nurtures local farmers, fresh local food sources, and which honors the human beings and, as well, the health of what monks would refer to as God's Creation.

It is clear that some monks and some Benedictine and other monastic communities have never given a thought to these questions. Others certainly have, as Benedictine monastics and as thinking human beings.

ECOLOGICALLY RELEVANT PRINCIPLES

Fr. Hugh Feiss, O.S.B., of Ascension Abbey in Idaho, cited earlier, is an important voice for monasticism and ecology. In his essay, "Water, Oneness and the West: Benedictine Theological Reflections," he lists seven monastic principles that are especially relevant to ecology:

- That the monastery have all the necessities within the enclosure, including water;

- That local specificity be observed and recognized, including a sufficient knowledge of local nature so that the monks might adapt to the place rather than forcing the place to adapt to them; a willingness to make do with what their neighbors do, not simply in terms of what is available in the neighborhood, but also what is produced there (siding much more with the local organic farmer than the industrial food and clothing providers); and the vow of stability as a tie to a very specific place and, with that, a commitment to thinking about the next generations;

- That the community accept personal and collective responsibility;

- That the community regard the sacramentality which is present, in the tools of the monastery which should be regarded with the same reverence as the vessels of the altar, and that they extend this sacramentality to animals and to elements of nature like water;

- An acceptance that conversion is continuous, that there be a willingness to learn and grow, to let go of what no longer works (Big organizations have great difficulty doing this, says Fr. Feiss—monasteries should not);

- A sense of compunction, tears, and contrition that we are creatures who pollute, damage, and destroy out of our lack of reverence for God's Creation;

- The sense of oneness with all things, for those who see things from the standpoint of God or in relation to God, all appears interconnected—Benedict's mystic experience implies the oneness of the Earth.

These principles, Fr. Feiss claims, call for conservation, for sustainable agriculture, for eating local foods and less meat, for living ecologically.[56]

IN PRACTICE—SOME CASE STUDIES

It is now time to look at some specific monastic communities and their effort and work in this area. Since some such communities have a college or university associated with them, it is important to first acknowledge that there are some perceived differences between a monastic higher education environment and a monastic environment. Interestingly, each suspects the other has it better. The monastic higher education environment, I have found, has more people, more labor, more help, and a wider range of same, than does the pure monastic environment. However, I have found the monastic higher education environment busier, more wrapped up in its ongoing work, potentially somewhat less creative and generally more cautious and conservative, albeit with more opportunity for good work. This characteristic somewhat parallels the cautious conservative nature of almost all institutions of higher education, private or public, religious affiliated or not: they are essentially conservators and transmitters of the culture, even when the culture is wrong, is bad, is no longer congruent with reality. An exclusive monastic environment with no affiliation with an educational institution has fewer people to draw from, is dominated more by individual personalities, is more role-oriented with departments and duties that can be sacrosanct and, albeit with fewer people, has a chance for more freedom and greater creativity. Leadership and the personality of leadership is likely more important in pure monastic community. Leadership is much more watered down and hard to pinpoint in a monastic/education environment. In general, religious communities without schools, whether monastic or otherwise, are potentially less conservative and more liberal and perhaps even somewhat radical, the very opposite of what some might expect.

The Monastery of St. Benedict in St. Joseph, Minnesota, and its associated College of Saint Benedict, stands as a strong example of ecological and very progressive values, even though it is of the higher education/monastic breed. The nuns of this large women's community, among the larger such Benedictine communities in the nation, are very much associated with the thinking of Thomas Berry, Wendell Berry, Wes Jackson, David Orr, Hildegard of Bingen, Winona LaDuke, and other important eco-philosophers, and these thinkers are not foreign to at least some of the college's course programs as well. This is revelatory of the spirit of the community, as is the college's heroic effort to "feminize" the very male-oriented science of chemistry. Both reveal much about the institution. There is a very active Community Supported Agriculture (CSA) project involving both the monastery and the college as members, along with the public, and involving student interns as well. There is strong direct involvement in a locally and largely organically certified farmers market, and, as well, encouragement and assistance to the regional and statewide farm community to organize and support such projects as a way to keep farmers on the land. The College of Saint Benedict has organized environmental conferences with strong eco-justice values, and the overall community and its leadership are very strong on principles of sustainability of both ecosystems and local community. The community oversees and manages, with emphasis on protection, preservation, and restoration, (the latter possible through the presence of the college and the technical assistance and labor it has to offer) about five hundred acres in woods, prairie, wetland, and leased cropland, assisted by college work/study students. The community garden at Saint Ben's provides food to both the CSA and the farmers market. There is a sizable "contemplative woodland" of maple, basswood, ironwood, and some oak, a source

of great pride to the nuns. No cutting is allowed. There are specific ecological restoration projects in wetland, prairie, and oak savanna. There
are also community gardens for the monks and some food production for
the monastery. Grapes are also grown in this CSA which has thirty-six
shareholders plus three charities as recipients. In addition to students,
labor needs are filled by two court-assigned "sentenced-to-serve" labor-
ers. The whole community is seriously involved in recycling for sale to
market and to farm application. There is a ministry of major external activism here, in agriculture, environment, land trust, and land protection
organizations, and in the promotion of farmers markets, across the region
and the state. There are also active applications to funding organizations
for specific projects, and strong mission and goals statements guiding all.

The nuns of Saint Benedict make clear and strong connections between their extensive ecological practices and their monastic spirituality.
Sr. Phyllis Plantenberg, O.S.B., speaks of the importance of prayer at the
appointed hours but clearly also recognizes the connection of work as
prayer. Noting the coincidence of Christian feasts with earlier pagan
worship, she notes the importance of the solstice and equinox celebrations which are observed at the monastery. She believes it is important
that we make time, that we mark our life; that gardening is marking the
growth of plants, that time is sacred, that it's a tool, a vessel, and that it's
violated, for the modern world does not see time as a gift. Likewise, she
and her sister nuns see land as precious, that we should seriously accept
our stewardship responsibilities, which includes love and community as
well as the land, and that we should live off our own bioregion, meaning, she says, that everyone needs to have a garden and a root cellar. Sr.
Phyllis finds that the Benedictine rule to honor the "sacrality of the utensils" stands in direct opposition to our designed obsolescence, and that
consumerism destroys our idea of both utensils and sacrality. Sr. Phyllis
and her associates demonstrate a charism and an approach to Benedictine spirituality which is very open, liberal, ecumenical, and easy. It is
also infused with a deep sense of bioregionalism and, as well, an openly
strong desire to link indigenous peoples' spirituality with Christianity.[57]

The brother monastic community of St. John's Abbey and University lies just a few miles away. Here one finds a sizable forest of old
growth and also well-managed timber and natural woodland, big enough
to fulfill all of the furniture needs of the entire monastery and university,
processed in the university's own woodworking shop. The monks practice a 100-year cutting rotation, ensuring a high quality managed forest.

On their fifty-acre prairie, they are engaged in a thusfar ten-year-old prairie restoration project, and an additional two-year-old project (both on three year burning rotations), plus a prairie wetland restoration, and an oak—savanna restoration, all on a total acreage of twenty-five hundred acres. They tap their maple trees for sugar, operate a sugar shack to produce maple syrup, protect ancient oak natural areas, and hope to acquire additional farmland to keep it in farming. To these monks of one of the largest abbeys in the United States, frugality, a sense of place, and their vow of stability are all important. They have a very strong ethic of sustainability and teach it within courses. At the monastery, they are also very interested in wind energy, a subject which raises some aesthetic concerns in the community (i.e., wind towers), although the Abbot, Fr. John Klassen, comments that, while we can't see the CO_2 in the air from all our fossil fuel burning, it's killing our woods and our environment.[58] There is clearly a less than perfect recycling system (and ethic?) here, but ecological restoration (especially prairie restoration) and natural resource management on the grounds are clearly central and are a powerful symbol as a key to the practice of Benedictine spirituality.

Out on the western North Dakota prairies stand side by side two Benedictine monasteries, one of which, Sacred Heart, has already been described in detail. Assumption Abbey is the other, known for its large agricultural operation (2,000 acres, with beef cattle on the open range, a dairy herd, a few horses, ducks and geese, but no other livestock currently). This monastery also has a very large vegetable garden, a lovingly cared for and mature afforestation project, and much acreage in grains for animal feed (oats, barley, hay). From their gardens, they put up, can, and pickle a great supply of food, an important element of overwintering in this remote area. They compost food waste and organic matter, likely more out of tradition than out of an ecological ethic, but have no land management plan; no resource or energy assessment on the buildings; no specific formal attempts at sustainability or ecological concern, in the food service or elsewhere, albeit an underlying and laid back deep frugality, very much in keeping with Benedictine monasticism, leads to some inherently ecological behavior. This monastery on the plains is the home of Fr. Terrence Kardong, O.S.B., perhaps the strongest Benedictine writer in the United States on questions of ecology and land stewardship. Due to Fr. Kardong's efforts, the monastery has been involved long-term in the environmental work of the Dakota Resource Council. Many of the characteristics cited earlier as challenges for contemporary monasteries, including the inheritance of very large and energy wasteful "old clunker" buildings, are typical of this monastery. Here also, as elsewhere, more ecologically sensitive younger monks are awaiting their opportunity to help their community in these endeavors. So, Assumption Abbey has its challenges. In providing a creativity-conducive setting, however, and over many long years, to one of the most ecologically important minds within monasticism in North America, Terrence Kardong, and to nurture and support him in many ways over so many long years, is no small feat and should not be minimized. The very high frugality and sense of communalism extant at Assumption Abbey provides a lesson that ecological wisdom and practice can come from other more implicit directions. Nevertheless, the men of Assumption could learn much from the women of Sacred Heart as to the more ecologically sensitive proper way of following the Rule of Benedict in the twenty-first century.[59]

The Benedictine Monastery of Osage in Oklahoma has a special characteristic that inures itself to ecological thought and behavior and to eco-justice: it is oriented to Eastern philosophy and has within it a special interest in and affinity for the inherently ecological interface of Christianity and Hinduism, of Christianity and Buddhism, of Christianity and other Asian religions. Greatly inspired by the life, work, and teaching of Fr. Bede Griffiths, O.S.B., an English Benedictine, who spent most of his life in India and worked at the Christian—Eastern interface, Osage Monastery is a central location in the United States (together with the Immaculate Conception/Big Sur Benedictine Monastery in California) for not only the distribution of Bede Griffiths' teachings, but also it contains an extensive library of Fr. Bede's works. Given this openness to Asian-based non-Western philosophy and religion, it will not surprise the visitor to see also at Osage a distinct openness toward and interest in American Indian spirituality and the ecological thought that goes with it. The chapel at Osage is sunken circular in style much like a southwestern Indian kiva. It is open to outdoors and to nature through extremely large windows (walls of glass), with a beautiful old growth scrub oak forest which fully surrounds the chapel and main community building. One notices American Indian feathers, drums, and other objects, combined with Asian floral and candle arrangements, involving many candles that one might see in an ashram (holy place) in India. One also notices that many of the monastic religious services are infused with Asian form, including an Eastern-style reverential bow with hands folded in place of a kiss or handshake of peace. The Eastern flame ceremony, which is an Asian ceremony but with close linkage to American Indian ritual, is also practiced. Both Asian and American Indian wall hangings and symbols are present in the chapel, as well as Asian crystals. In the liturgies, Eastern readings from the Bhagavad-Gita and the Tao te Ching are interspersed with Western Christian readings. A photo of the Pope and the Dalai Lama together in one picture is displayed. Outdoors there is a Zen garden with a printed guide available. The message here is the combination of a non-Western culture and a strong nature and earth-based philosophy, Asian and North American, at one with Christianity. (One gets the feeling here that Thomas Berry, historian of East Asian religion and philosopher of eco-spirituality and American Indian wisdom, would feel very much at home in this place.)

Outside at Osage there is a heavy and central emphasis on the carefully constructed and maintained trails on the monastery's forty-three acres. These trails are not a minor addition, but are central to meditation, prayer, centering, recreation, and refreshment; they reflect a strong sense of nature appreciation, and of nature mysticism. Meals are mainly vegetarian, as one might expect, for spiritual and ecological reasons (in spite of the fact that culturally this is beef and cattle country).[60]

Al Fritsch, the Jesuit ecological ethicist and resource assessor, completed a detailed resource inventory/assessment of Osage a few years ago, at the request of the monastic sisters and in conjunction with all their other communities in other states. He wrote of Osage: "The uniqueness of this ministry makes comparison with other monastic outreach programs quite difficult."[61] In this community, there is very little agricultural land or food production, although there is a strong composting system for kitchen and food waste. While the community's food must be entirely brought in from outside, this monastery scores extremely high on energy priorities, with very little room for improvement. This standard also holds for recycling (of virtually everything), strong water conservation, no air conditioning (in spite of very warm summer weather), and, as elsewhere in many monasteries, a strong ethic of frugality. They practice some ecological activism outside the monastery. Strong values of anticonsumption and social justice, and the linkage between the two, are present. The vision for Osage was of a small (model) community of women making a strong anticonsumption and nature-based statement, founded in Christian monastic tradition, with a strong interreligious Eastern flavor, open to Eastern spirituality and inspired by

Bede Griffiths, which they have largely achieved. Osage is an ecological community which doesn't know it's an ecological community. It is not perfect in all ways, especially with respect to food sources, but nevertheless it represents a high order of sustainable ecological living. Its values are inherently more countercultural than most, and it has high potential to be a center for the integration of Asian, Native American, and ecological thought in conjunction with Christianity. Its lack of symmetry with the contemporary culture of its region does not weaken its ability to maintain a strong sense of place, and with possibly a deeper philosophical and spiritual connection to where this land was situated not too long ago, in Indian Territory, and, before that, the land of the Osage and other Plains Indians.

Farther west on the West Texas High Plains and perched at the very edge of a canyon in the Caprock Canyonlands, one finds the Benedictine Monastery of St. Benedict. Another monastic community with strong ecological values and one much involved in activism oriented toward small farm and environmental issues, this community currently has only a small vegetable garden itself. Over the long term they will plant and manage buffalo grass for erosion control and to bar invasive species, of which they are very concerned. These women are also very proud of their recycled tire-based erosion control project at the canyon's edge. The atmosphere here is of great concern for small-scale farming and small farms, worry over greed-driven large-scale industrial agriculture, and with a strong distrust of genetic engineering. They have great respect for the agricultural and environmental philosophy of Wendell Berry, though with lesser knowledge of Thomas Berry. The monks of this small monastery are very involved regionally in the Promised Land Network (PLN) (see Social Justice/Eco-Justice chapter). This is another community of insufficient membership and a burden of too large overbuilt facilities, but one with great innate (more than acquired) ecological sustainability values.[62]

There are times when a monastery's physical circumstances, its natural affinities for frugality, stability, and a sense of place, result in a circumstance of ecological sustainability not otherwise intended and not based necessarily on ecological or sustainability values. The very remote Monastery of Christ in the Desert is a case in point. Located on a site chosen forty years ago for its very remoteness, Christ in the Desert has never been on the electrical grid, has never had telephone service, and has always been very difficult to get to (or from), for it is at the end of a long and poorly maintained U.S. Forest Service road in the beautiful Chama Canyon of western New Mexico. Since its siting a number of decades ago, the surrounding National Forest Land has been designated the Chama Wilderness, foreclosing any possibility of electrical service to the monastery (short of the expenditure of millions of dollars to bury the lines, and foreclosing also significant improvement in access). This reality has caused the monks to become very sophisticated with solar energy, including solar arrays which follow the sun. It has also caused a high order of energy conservation, highly insulated strawbale construction, passive as well as active solar gain, and an added encouragement to energy frugality, as well as other forms. The values here come from a response to necessity and reality rather than from an ecological value system. However, necessity and reality can also be a good reason to model ecologically desirable systems, as can a value system congruent with them. Due to these realities and the monks' response to them, these monastics have become somewhat expert in their solar technologies, in their strawbale and other building design and in other ways, and are sought after for their experience. (It should be mentioned that they do use a good deal of propane gas for energy, something that might change with a change in their value system.) Details of their technical response include significant and serious strawbale architecture, trombe walls, solar reflectors on skylights, extensive numbers of skylights, extensive solar storage batteries as well as sun-tracking technology. They also have constructed wetlands for both gray and black (sewage) water, producing a crop of thick reeds (which could be used as compost, but is not). They are employing the services of one of Santa Fe's very best solar and alternative energy architects, a subject of envy by others outside the community. Water conservation plays a role, too, in this dry desert environment, although their site immediately adjacent to a large and always flowing river reduces the immediate necessity and makes it a question of more electricity (energy) conservation than water conservation.[63]

There were early plans for large-scale agriculture at the Monastery of Christ in the Desert, including irrigation infrastructure in the lower fields adjacent to the river, but these plans, along with a goat herd, were abandoned some time ago. Food to the monastery comes from conventional industrial (and nonecological) sources, and the value system has departed so far from ecology relative to food sustenance that the monks are even thinking of selling some of their water rights (which, should it happen, would likely be an irreversible decision). A few of the monks here see the connection of food as a moral choice, for eating is a moral act, to quote the National Catholic Rural Life Conference; they accept that such belief should be natural for Benedictine communities, but unfortunately, monastic passivity reigns. Thus, a questionable value system on food and agriculture, and a value system on energy and design driven as a consequence of necessity rather than good ecological values gives this extremely beautiful and exceedingly remote wilderness monastery a mixed record.

There is some variation from monastery to monastery in the number of times per twenty-four hour cycle that the monks gather in chapel for community prayer. Those monastic communities, which gather more frequently (perhaps seven or even eight times per day and night), do not have the time, energy or, I would say, inclination, to provide for their own needs, and are much more likely to display a value system akin to mainstream society which ignores the social and ecological ramifications of one's (or the community's) lifestyle. Those communities which gather for communal prayer less frequently, perhaps four times per day, are far more likely to be aware of the impact of their lives on other people and on the ecosystem. These are the people who can accept work or labor as prayer, if carried out in a prayerful way, while the others take prayer in a more literal sense. These are the monks who have the energy, the time, and the inclination to live sustainably, to live ecologically, and to interpret the Rule of Benedict more literally. I would argue that the Rule of Benedict would clearly require time in chapel in communal prayer over time spent working to make products to sell, but that it is reasonable to assume that time spent in prayer in chapel should not destroy the possibility of the monastery's providing for its own food and other basic needs, especially when the alternative is complicity in a socially and ecologically destructive economic system of industrial agriculture and sweatshop labor. This is, however, for each community and each individual monk to decide. The question of a lack of farmers and gardening interest within the community is another issue, perhaps rectifiable in the near-term by seeking external lay assistance from those with the requisite skills and interests, and also by trying to get this lay help to teach the monks. The Monastery of Christ in the Desert suffers from the twin challenges of a substantial in-chapel schedule and a lack of farm or garden-oriented personnel within the community. But this monastery is not challenged by lack of potential.

Not all Christian monasteries are Benedictine. The Carmelites' Nada Hermitage at Crestone, Colorado, is well known for advanced energy conservation, alternative energy sources, highly efficient ecological building design, and a strongly ecologically oriented attitude toward the Creation. Trappist, or Cistercian monasteries are also found across the country, often with considerable land and a strong agricultural heritage. Our Lady of the Mississippi on the bluffs overlooking the Mississippi River in Iowa, is one example, with a strong record of certified organic agriculture for some decades (hay, corn, beans, oats).[64] These Trappist (Cistercian) monks are knowledgeable about organic-agronomic systems, about organic-certification standards, and even about markets for their dairy-based products (chocolates, mainly). They continue to rent out pastureland (as many monasteries do), albeit with ecological oversight, and practice Holistic Resource Management (HRM) grazing techniques, producing only a very high quality product. (These monks have lately been searching their region for non-BST milk and organic milk, and are beginning to set the standard in their region for high quality and progressive ecological agriculture. They combine their agricultural initiatives, particularly grazing, with the nearby Trappist Monastery of New Melleray (a much larger monastery and larger agricultural operation but not nearly as ecologically enlightened—Our Lady of the Mississippi leads in this way), and with the nearby nonmonastic Dominican Motherhouse of Sinsinawa, which has had strong agricultural ministries of an ecological kind but which is now retreating from leadership in this area.

The women of Our Lady of the Mississippi also conduct active management of woodlands and timber stand improvement, have a large vegetable garden and fruit orchard, a prairie in restoration, a strongly supportive position on assisting women in agriculture, strong organizing on GMO and organic agriculture questions, and activity searching for and supporting markets for organic product. They farm 450 acres, and manage another 550 acres of woodland. This is a bright, young, energetic, and committed farming community with enlightened and progressive ecological values, strongly oriented to organic agriculture, and with a clear realization of the repercussions of the nation's cheap food policy.

The Cistercian monks of New Melleray, just to the west, have three thousand acres (1,800 tillable and 1,200 in forest), with many pastures that have returned to woodland.[65] Like many monasteries, they were fully food self-sufficient in their large community and in their large guesthouse as recently as the 1950s. Today, they remain self-sufficient in potatoes and 50 percent self-sufficient in vegetables, plus a lot of freezing of food product. After going through a typical period of agricultural decline in the 1960s and 1970s, they toyed with large-scale agri-business philosophy but have now reversed that direction and are rapidly becoming organic. They sell sweet corn, after providing for their own needs, and provide mixed vegetables to food pantries. They're very big on crop rotation, companion planting, and intercropping, receiving wood, leaves, and garden waste for compost from the nearby City of Dubuque, and are actively resisting accepting sludge (from Dubuque), GMOs (which they refer to as the "devil's workshop"), and confined livestock (hog) concentrations nearby. They may return to grass-fed beef cattle production. Symptomatic of the times, their abandonment of livestock and crop diversification in the 1960s–1970s led to a short-term embrace of industrial agriculture in what they call "de-hy," that is the dehydration of alfalfa into pellets, supposedly the magic elixir for the survival of their farm and community. They learned something from that experience, given their new directions today. A few decades ago, these Cistercians did make very progressive strides in alternative energy and are proud of their wood chip gasification plant. This was state of the art energy technology twenty years ago, and allows burning of wood with 75 percent moisture content. The monastery gets nearly free chips from the great number of wood pallets disposed of by the city of Dubuque (in lieu of landfill and high tipping fees for the city). This is much cheaper for the monastery than any other heating alternative (so there was a strong economic component rather than an ecological one, for the original decision), but there are no pollutant emissions (only steam and water vapor, with very little ash). (They received a 100 percent payback on their investment in just four years!) They now have so much energy that, although there's interest in wind turbines here, there's just no need for more energy. (The monks are, however, employing solar-powered fences and deer chasers for animal control to protect their nut trees and field crops.) Strong leadership at the monastery with a commitment to ecological and sustainable agriculture values is responsible for the changes in direction at the monastery as well as effective external cooperation and activism; it is a testament to the idea that the qualities and values of leadership in these hierarchical institutions is of critical importance.

CHALLENGES

Leadership changes. There is also turnover of monks in the community (in spite of the vow of stability) because individuals, including those key to energy, agricultural, and sustainability directions, sometimes leave the community (or die) and are not easily replaceable. (Monasteries do not advertise for certain types of people or skills, they take what they get. Thus, it is not uncommon to have a complete lack of skills in some areas, regardless of values or interests.) It is also true, however, that the place takes on the quality of the people who live there, and places do tend to attract like-minded individuals. This provides a recipe for great progress in the ecological and sustainability direction. Or it can provide a recipe for disaster. And there are monastic communities that demonstrate little or nothing to commend them to the directions of this volume, monasteries which would be no more attuned to ecological wisdom or sustainability than would be the mainstream of our very unecological, even antiecological, and unsustainable society and culture. Such places might even be so far removed in their thinking in these directions that they would wonder why anyone would equate them with ecology. Or, they might be so naïve about ecology as to claim to embrace all the values discussed in this book, and all the linkages to monastic spirituality and to Christianity, and live and behave as if they believe none of them. Our values are demonstrated by the way in which we live on a daily basis, and not on what we say, or what we claim them to be. There is nothing automatic about any connection or alleged connection between monasteries and ecological sustainability.

There is, of course, the question of separation from their apostolate, the problem of duality. If a monastic community or individual monks are doing things out of curiosity or necessity, but make no connection between this and their reason for being monks (or professed religious), then their work will be too shallow to survive. This is the case at a monastery which has what was once referred to as the greatest passive solar building in the nation, and, in addition, a lot of fame for energy conservation, so much so that they became a model for others. But, never connecting this to their apostolate, to their faith belief, to moral choice, or to the teachings of their religion, such effort must today be regarded as a failure. Another monastic community that achieved much positive notoriety for its land stewardship measures also lives today on past glory, for those measures at best were based on a sense of good citizenship and, at worst, a desire for image, a desire to be noticed, and not on any sense of moral imperative or accountability, not on any spiritual or theological sense. Likewise, such efforts pass into history and the contemporary community is deserving of no credit for such values. There are monasteries that are as crass as the worst examples one can find in the lay society when it comes to questions of food, (which can be very poor in quality, as well as coming from ecologically questionable sources), energy, recycling, stewardship, waste disposal, and their preaching which displays no realization or sensitivity to such matters (and which may be defensive as well). Sometimes there's a question of poor leadership, in which case monks with strong values in these areas can be tolerated at best but, as often, denigrated and marginalized. There is often little or no sense of place in such monasteries, and one may seriously wonder how they interpret the Rule of Benedict or other monastic rule by which they may be governed. And since like people attract like people, whether as religious members of the community, oblates (lay associates), or lay visitors, such places attract people with poorly developed social justice and eco-justice values who really wouldn't want to engage in dialogue about the matter and who might behave quite defensively. Theologically, such communities are likely to place transcendence (God apart, God removed, up on high, but not with us on Earth) over immanence (the much more ecological theological tenet of God in all, God everywhere, the Creator in the created), enabling them to be much less sensitive to ecological (or perhaps even social) concerns around them, and sometimes even ecologically destructive. Having a low regard for immanence, such monks have little regard for sacrality of place, sacrality of physical things, and a very weak sense of place, biotically, ecologically, or culturally, all in contrast to the Rule of Benedict. They attract like-minded people around them. A connection, therefore, between monasteries and ecology or sustainability, or even stewardship, is not automatic, in spite of the Rule of Benedict and similar monastic rules. For numerous reasons discussed heretofore, however, there is substance to the idea and ideal that Christian monasteries, countercultural as they can be, could serve as models of spiritually grounded sustainability.

If the religious and spiritual precepts and practices focused upon in this and preceding chapters are to be understood in the contemporary world, they must be seen as integral with modern science, and with scientific mystery. And we must ask the question can we be led to them through that scientific mystery. That is the focus of the following chapter.

Chapter Seven

ON SCIENCE

People involved in and committed to spiritually grounded sustainability are strong celebrants of science. Thus, a chapter on their view of science is critical to any understanding of this form of commitment to sustainability.

A basic premise here is that a spirituality that encourages ecological practice must be compatible with the best available science of the day. And that science is not the old and outmoded Cartesian-Baconian-Newtonian paradigm, the system and assumptions developed by René Descartes, Nathaniel Bacon, and Sir Isaac Newton, but rather the new story of quantum theory and ecology, of wholism rather than reductionism.[1] According to Terrence Kardong: ". . . (T)he most revolutionary discoveries in science have come in quantum physics, for here the Newtonian Age has truly come to an end."[2] What has been discovered is truly extraordinary: the basic reality of the universe is change, not stasis.

The first principle of ecology, that all is connected to all, in fact changes all in our view of scientific reality. The knowledge from quantum physics that every atom is immediately present to and influencing every other atom in the universe without passing through the intervening space, changes all the rules, alters in the most fundamental way possible, our understanding of reality.

The philosophy of science required by ecological thought and an understanding and acceptance of ecological principle is a philosophy of science which deeply questions the continuing validity of the four hundred year old Cartesian-Newtonian-Baconian approach to nature, to reality, the approach which has been so dominant, so influential and so

largely unquestioned until quite recently. The reality of ecology, the evolutionary development of twentieth-century quantum physics/quantum
mechanics, and the humbling nature of recent discoveries in science all
support the antireductionistic, antilinear, antimechanical view of science
with which we have become so familiar. To understand the nature of reality at the nexus of sustainability and spirituality, to understand the assumptions, the world view and the interpretation of nature and natural
reality held by the spiritually driven and faith-based communities described in this volume, one must consider the implications of ecology, of
the new discoveries in physics, and the humbling lessons taught by recent
developments in our understanding of nature. For some this will seem a
radical departure. With the support of such understanding, however, we
can begin to understand what will be necessary if the models of sustainability described in this book are to be of value to us.

   A most common and popular view of dinosaurs is to think of them
as primitive, stupid, pea-brained, and a failed category of life that became
extinct long, long ago. There is an implication in their extinction story
that they were somehow unable to adapt and thus met their demise. Such
thinking derives from human arrogance and hubris more than from any
real evidence, but it is perhaps worth realizing that dinosaurs lived from
225 million years ago to their extinction 160 million years later. (Some
believe they are at least partially still with us in the form of birds.) The
best thinking on the age of human beings is three million years, and perhaps as much as four. By this measure, human beings are exceedingly
young and largely untested compared to their much, much longer evolved
dinosaur brethren, being on the planet thusfar a mere four-tenths of
1 percent of the time allotted to dinosaurs. How little, how minuscule we
are compared to what we like to think! And there is some suggestion that
our own days remaining toward extinction may be forseeable given our
global environmental challenges.

   Thanks to ever-developing new technology and the normally to be
expected scientific discovery, we have recently made some not surprising
but nevertheless extraordinary scientific discoveries of a conventional
type, which we should continue to expect in the future. For example, recently we have just become aware that human life on Earth in the form of
Homo erectus (essentially modern hominids) is now known to be at least
three million years on Earth rather than the until recently believed two
million years. Further, we now know that our ancestors dispersed from
their origin in Africa some two million rather than one million years ago.

Further, thanks to the Hubble spacecraft and its observational abilities, we have confirmed the discovery of not only new planets, but also new planets in solar systems other than our own. This is truly an extraordinary discovery we should not be taking lightly for it increases the odds of extraterrestrial life and, together with the new knowledge of *Homo erectus*, should not only give us pause, but should lead us to a much humbler state than has been our wont. These are only discoveries of conventional science but should nevertheless take us down a peg or two in our self-assessment of what we know or think we know, either about life or about the universe.

Perhaps much more significant in the very recent past has been the discovery in the Baltic Sea off the coast of Denmark of *Symbion pandora*. What is *Symbion pandora*? *S. pandora* is a small animal organism visible to the naked eye living on the mouth part of a Baltic Sea lobster. It represents a whole new phylum of animal life, of which there are only about twenty-nine such phyla known in the world. How can it be that a whole new phyla existed, visible to the naked eye, in an anything but remote location near a modern scientific country which has experienced the full force of modern scientific observation and analysis for hundreds of years? Did some new technology bring this about by giving us stronger observational powers? Not at all. *S. pandora* was there all the time. Perhaps it could be argued that we did not see it because we were not prepared to see it. We were not looking for it and suffered a typical human trait, the limitation of blindness, of lack of perception, of lack of a mind open to receive. In its way, this discovery is more humbling than either the age of hominids, or the discovery of planets in a solar system other than our own, for it was there in front of our eyes all along and required the development of no new technology for its discovery. Another most humbling discovery and a true celebration of the revelation of Nature.

We speak of the "laws of physics" or "laws of biology" and assign to them a degree of rigidity which they do not deserve. What are we to make of such supposedly immovable laws when we witness a school of fish, a flock of birds, or perhaps a herd of pronghorn defying these "laws" with instantaneous and fully coordinated change of direction, in violation not only of physics, but also of biological behavior and of mental or instinctive response time? How much do we really know?

It was reported in the British journal *Nature* and in the *New York Times Science Section*, but not widely anywhere else, that life (in microbiological form) exists in the earth itself (not simply in soil, in caves, or in the deep sea but in the bedrock, in the geologic mass of the planet down to a depth of at least three miles, perhaps more). We also know that the sum total of this life within earth, the biotic mass of this life, is greater than the sum total of the biotic mass of life, plant, and animal, to be found on the planet's surface. Even more extraordinary, we know that this life evolved disconnected from and on an entirely different evolutionary path from the evolution of that on the surface, the two being separated for quite a few million years. Perhaps the most significant aspect of this discovery is the long-term conviction of modern science that such life did not and could not exist. Until the time of discovery, modern science was not simply ignorant of the existence of such life but categorically said it could not exist, that, in fact, it did not exist. Not having any definitive grounds for such a position, science was behaving quite unscientifically in categorically denying the possibility. There was, of course, no earlier knowledge of evidence for the existence of such life, but there was also no way of proving that such life did not or could not exist. (Similarly, to say that life does not exist on Mars is not a scientific statement, for it cannot be proven. To say that there is no evidence to support the existence of life on Mars is a correct and scientifically based statement.) Such is further evidence of the wonder of nature, the limits of science, and the ever present need to control human arrogance.

The Indian-born, Western-trained scientist Vandana Shiva, a nuclear physicist and analyst of Third World agriculture, forestry, and women-in-development, is known for her oft-quoted belief that there is Western science and there are other ways of knowing. The statement, coming from one trained in Western science, acknowledges Western science as a legitimate way of knowing. And yet the statement is heretical to Western science which does not grant legitimacy to any other way of knowing. Since Western science, a valid way of knowing, cannot categorically deny the possibility that there are or might be other ways of knowing, the correct behavior of Western science would be to acknowledge rather than to deny the possibility. Because Western science denies that possibility, it is not itself scientific; it reveals its own insecurity and its own limitations. To say that Western science is the only way of knowing is unscientific by the very definition of Western science.

Further humbling to our psyche is the realization that whoever we are as humans is, evolutionarily, far more whoever it is we have become in many thousands, even tens of thousands of years, of prewritten history, in comparison to the mere five thousand years or so of written history. There were far more human generations (and thus opportunity for adaptation and evolution) in that long period of time than have occurred in the latter few thousand years of recorded history, that little portion of our history about which we know something. This is further evidence about how little we know, about how little we can possibly know, about ourselves as a species, about who we are, where we have come from, and where we are going.

When one adds to this catalog of limits to our science and to what we can know or not know, the natural tendency is to distort science due to the nature of human character. We don't want to admit to a science, to a world view, to a way of knowing which is indeed so limited. Like anything else in life, science is distorted and/or corrupted in its task through money, cultural blinders, through power and control, and what all these things do to the human psyche, dictating at the very least what work proceeds and what work does not proceed, what questions are asked and, equally if not more importantly, what questions are not asked. The capture of American physicists by the defense industry and of biologists by the biotechnology/genetic engineering industry are two prominent examples of this distortion. They lead science through money and power toward certain areas and directions and distinctly away from others, and they are further serious contributors to scientific limitation and to the danger inherent in the notion that Western science is the only way of knowing.

All of the foregoing points to a perhaps more proper attitude toward Nature, toward science. Such would be an attitude much more deeply inspired by awe, by a sense of wonder, by the revelation of nature as a jaw-dropping experience, rather than the mechanical business-as-usual experience we have taken it for in modern times. And all of it points to the practice of science as inherently limited and as just that, a practice, an approach, a way of knowing, based on a methodology (commonly called the "scientific method") and/or peer review of both its findings and its methodology. We must not take it for more, or we weaken or perhaps even destroy its ability to serve. Perhaps our very use of the word "science" has invited trouble due to the way in which we use it. We fail to acknowledge its limitations and we place it upon a pedestal from which the only path is down. Perhaps we should return to the original name for science, namely, "nature," or even the older and much maligned phrase "natural history," leaving for "science" purely the approach, or approaches, to the study of

Nature and natural history. This puts science, which is a practice, into proper context.

Thomas Berry has something to teach us here. Berry has said that, in the phenomenal order, the universe is the only text without a context. All else is, and must be treated, in context. This is precisely the lesson of ecology.

As most now know, ecology is the study of "*oikos*," the home, our home, the only home we have. It is the study of Earth, including ourselves and our place in context within and as a functioning part of Earth. The very important principles of ecology, as we recall from earlier in this volume, might be put forth as:

1. Everything is connected to every other thing.

2. Nature knows best.

3. Everything must go somewhere.

4. There's no such thing as a free lunch.

This popularization of ecology's basic principles is a comprehensive portrayal of the science of ecology, a science which is given broad lip service by modern society, but which is done so by a society that will not or cannot live or behave ecologically. Ecology is radical and revolutionary by any reasonable interpretation of the way of modern life. Ecology has been referred to as the "subversive science" because it undercuts or subverts most conventional reductionistic science as it has developed in modern times. Ecology is holistic (the popular spelling although meaning dictates the proper spelling should be "wholistic" since we are speaking of "holism," not "holes"). Ecology is integral and antireductionistic. None of these characterize the dominant or conventional strain of the remainder of modern science. Ecology does not stand in contrast to but rather is in synchrony with the mid- to late-twentieth-century findings of quantum physics, quantum mechanics, and chaos theory in mathematics. All of the latter bring into sharp question the three to four century-old assumptions of Cartesian, Newtonian, and Baconian thinking, thinking which assumes all is mechanistic, that all functions like a machine. So, we are suffering here from the flaws and blinders of Cartesian-Newtonian-Baconian thought and, quite naturally, find it difficult to let go, and to accept the unknown.

The twentieth century contribution to the science of Heisenberg's "Uncertainty Principle" has had a profound influence in changing our perception of and attitude toward science and of what we can and should expect from scientific investigation. The realization of this principle can have no less than a profoundly fundamental impact on the direction of our science and the role science will play in the future. There is no objectivity in science, and we are not separated from that which we observe. Our very study or observation of phenomena changes those phenomena. We have known for some time that we are not fully objective observers of history, society, ethics, religion, or philosophy. Now we know we are not, and, as well, cannot be objective observers of the natural sciences or Nature or natural history—it simply isn't possible. Natural science is no longer separated from social science or the humanities. Heisenberg's Uncertainty Principle, that whatever one studies one changes, is a revelation from the "hardest" and most rigid of the "hard sciences," physics, and is now a part of all science. Nothing can be the same as it was in the Cartesian era of the last four centuries. It is now ever to be understood: the whole is greater than the sum of its parts. We are launched in a new direction. This realization alone might justify the notion of a "New Age."

Much of the foregoing would be natural if we became re-enchanted with the natural order, with something bigger and beyond our own mere selves. What if we accepted and became open to the Cartesian critique? What if we accepted Western-trained Indian physicist Vandana Shiva's comment "There is Western science and there are other ways of knowing?" Our world would be a different place.

Einstein has lived. So has Heisenberg, Ilya Prigogine, Gregory Bateson, David Bohm, Barry Commoner, Rene Dubos, Sir James Lovelock, Brian Swimme, Heinz Pagels, Rupert Sheldrake, and many other twentieth-century scientists. For that, the world will not, indeed, cannot be the same.

We know that three and a half centuries ago René Descartes, Sir Isaac Newton, and Francis Bacon gave us a view of science, a world view, which has dominated and governed us ever since. Perhaps it could be said that that world view derived naturally, given events which preceded it. And it certainly spread well beyond Western society and culture to encompass the globe. And, functionally, it still dominates today. But the likelihood of its continued ability to survive is small in light of what we have now come to understand about science, about Nature, about the nature of reality, about what and how we know, about who we are, about the cosmos and its evolutionary process, cosmogenesis. These have changed all that has gone before. If, as Thomas Berry and Brian Swimme have told us, that, in the phenomenal order, the universe itself is the only text without a context, our view of ecology is forever broadened. And, as Berry and Swimme have also related, it is the unique role of the human being to serve in the role of the universe reflecting upon itself. We are engaging in serious reflection in these areas, tackling the deepest ecological, scientific, philosophical, and theological questions which could ever be posed to us. These questions are based upon deeply profound realities: all things are related to, interdependent upon, and therefore part of all other things (the first principle of ecology); the observer cannot separate from the observed, thus ultimately there can be no objectivity (Heisenberg's Uncertainty Principle); and all reality is not only relational and contextural but also, at its core, process (the lessons of quantum physics/quantum mechanics). (One is tempted here to add the revelations of chaos theory in mathematics, useful in humbling us, but also suggesting an underlying order to chaos. However, this order demands far superior technology than is available to us if we are to understand it, perhaps a technology which would never become available as the goal of understanding always recedes to the horizon.)

We have spent many years thinking about Newton's apple falling from the tree, and have designed the whole science of physics around it. What if Newton and we had concentrated more on how the apple got up into the tree in the first place, then what kind of physics would we have? And what place ecology?

We are also given, at the beginning of the twenty-first century, the renewed conviction (which as humans we once had but lost) that Nature is revelatory. Nature is a basic guide or teacher. Such is not to deny the existence of other teachers or revelation in our lives, whether books of wisdom, Holy Scripture, or our own intuition or inner voice, but to emphasize the great denial of Nature as teacher, Nature as revelatory, which we have engaged in since the advent of the Enlightenment, if not before. ("Nature knows best" is, in fact, the second major ecological principle.)

Religion, spirituality, the presence of human wisdom and experience also serves as teacher and guide. The wisdom of the East teaches us that ecological principles are necessary but not sufficient, as we are called upon to give back more than we take, from the planet or from one another; to give something of ourselves to future generations; and to recognize the need to replenish and renew ourselves, our spirit, our souls. According to Eastern thought, therefore, replacement, or leaving something (i.e., the planet) as good as we found it is not enough. We must improve it. This thinking suggests that, in truth, we are far removed from any sustainability ethic.

A 1989 interview with physicist David Bohm at the Niels Bohr Institute in Copenhagen reveals a scientific philosophy strikingly congruent with indigenous (non-Western) peoples' approach to reality, and congruent as well with Thomas Berry's "new story."[3] In that interview, Bohm relates the new world view as having a focus on wholeness and process rather than on parts and constituents. Evidence for this new world view in physics is coming primarily from new discoveries in quantum theory, and secondarily from relativity. Bohm refers to relativity as a notion of a universal field, an unbroken universe, in constant flow. He sees the concept of space and time as relative and views that as truly revolutionary. Bohm further explains that quantum theory has three main features:

- the notion that a quantum process is indivisible, that each process is a whole, that all quantum movements are linked into one whole;

- the notion that waves and particles are interrelated, can behave like one another, are not intrinsic, and depend on context;

- the notion of non-locality, which, combined with the others, suggests that the universe is an indivisible whole rather than being constructed of separate parts or constituent elements which interact.

Unity can create order, says Bohm.

Bohm finds that our perception is influenced by our way of thinking; hence, we see parts rather than wholes in physics because that's the way we're conditioned to think in modern times. If you go back one to two thousand years we wouldn't be thinking that way. Our mechanical way of thinking and looking is recent, Bohm says, for earlier people didn't see the parts as primary.

In classical physics, the part is the primary concept, parts are the basic reality, and the whole is only an auxiliary concept which is convenient. In holistic thinking, the whole is primary. Quantum mechanics teaches the whole is objective—we are the ones who make up the parts but the whole is fundamental.

What is the relationship of theory to reality? We don't like our world view to be questioned; we don't want to accept that all world views are limited. The need today is for a broader world view, for the Western world view focuses too much on analysis which leads it to fragmentation. If you try to break up reality falsely into fragments, you'll get confusion because you'll treat fragments separately when they're not separate. We inevitably confuse the part and the whole because we take a fragment as an independent whole. Further, the observer is an intrinsic part of the whole so you cannot get an unambiguous meaning to any measurement.

The medieval era's world view held that everything was analogous to everything else, that the human being was a microcosm of the whole so the human would have the possibility of understanding the whole. The Cartesian era brought on the fragmentation of Nature and by the 1930s physicists had a feeling for the critique of the fragmentary world view; they were the first to see it. This change opens the prospect for the inevitable reconnection of science and religion.

The philosopher of science Langdon Gilkey in his book, *Nature, Reality and the Sacred: The Nexus of Science and Religion*,[4] writes that a purely religious understanding of nature, void of any influence of science, is indefensible. Such is antithetical to all that modern inquiry knows about nature around us, and leaves nature empty of any real significance. And he writes that a purely scientific understanding of nature, void of any influence of religious understanding, is equally indefensible, although it is thoroughly dominant in our culture; it leads to thorough objectification. He concludes that a purely scientific understanding is more devastating than a purely religious understanding, because the scientific apprehension provides the intellectual legitimation for the industrial and commercial exploitation of nature. Gilkey's premise is that neither science nor religious apprehension alone can provide us with a definitive or exhaustive understanding of nature's power, creativity, and mystery. Both science and religion represent authentic expressions of the human response to nature and, if taken together, usher us into a new knowing of natural process and a new sense of nature's reality.

The word "science" and the word "why" should be synonymous. Science at its best involves the never-ending question of "Why?" and never stops asking that question in its endless search for reality, for truth. And yet much of what passes for science in our society and in our culture is sufficiently constrained as to raise the question of whether or not it might legitimately be called science. Additional to the pressure and resultant constraint coming from concentrated wealth and power fearful for its security and/or in search of reinforcement is the distinction inherent in the nearly four centuries of Cartesian and Newtonian reductionism. The latter is a significant disadvantage given twentieth-century discoveries in quantum physics/quantum mechanics, chaos theory in mathematics, and ecology.

Thus, the ultimate question for science is the "why" question, not the "how" question. To ask "how" is legitimate vis-à-vis science, but it is limited, narrow, constrained, and tends more toward mechanics and technology than to true science. It is only through asking "why," but "why," but "why," infinitely, that true science can be conducted.

The ultimate question in religion is also the "why?" question. Thus, religion and science are very much related and do not differ as much as we might like to think. The latter circumstance is admittedly uncomfortable for some.

Nature is revelatory. Revelation is not limited to the printed word, to books, to ideas, to pronouncements of human beings, or to Scripture. Revelation, indeed, can come from these sources, but it comes to us also from nature, from the natural order, from the world about us, from the universe, from the cosmos. Science is the humans' study of that revelation of nature. It is conducted with a certain methodology, the scientific method, a method based upon the reasoning process of the mind, and involves a control called "peer review and testing." Thus, it is disciplined. But it is also filled with mystery and is dependent upon human intuition and creativity for its ultimate success as science.

These approaches to a scientific world view are implicit in any serious treatment of ecology and religion, of sustainability and spirituality. They are, as well, implicit if not always explicit, in the belief system of practitioners described in the pages of this book. Humility and awe before the whole is key. In that humility and awe, science and religion are really not far apart.

Indigenous people, Native Americans in particular, find no separation between science and religion, between sustainability and spirituality. Perhaps this is a reason why spiritually based or faith-based practitioners of sustainability draw so heavily from indigenous people, particularly from the indigenes of our own continent.

Given the discoveries of the twentieth century outlined in this chapter, it is only through this broader awareness of the nature of things, of the nature of science, and of nature's ability to reveal, that true scientific progress will be made.

Science and religion are really not far apart, and the indigenous peoples' experience reenforces that notion.

The story is told of the American Indian who asks his white brother to look down at the ground at his feet. "What do you see?" asks the Indian. The white man responds, as expected: "soil, a few blades of grass, an insect or two, some pebbles." "Is that all you see?" asks the Indian. "Yes," says the white man, wondering if there's something he should see which he's not seeing. "Are you sure that's all you see?" asks the Indian. The white man is now getting irritated, beginning to wonder what this is all about. The Indian goes on with his questioning. "Do you not see what I see?" he asks. "When I look down I see, among the things you see, the faces of all those future generations yet to come, awaiting their turn."

In British filmmaker John Boorman's celebrated film, *The Emerald Forest*, there is a memorable scene of an Amazonian native, a Yanomami tribesman, watching giant bulldozers at work preparing the site for the construction of the huge Tucurui Dam in the Brazilian Amazon. As the machine removes the tropical rainforest and completely clears the site for construction, the Yanomami elder asks the question, "But how will the earth breathe?"

These two stories of Native American tribal experience are perfect expositions of ecological thought and principle. The Indian shows an awareness that he is not alone, that he is part of a much larger process, and that he has obligations toward future peoples (and creatures of all kinds) yet to come. I would argue, that this very much science-based approach has developed over long centuries of evolution. The first reveals ecological knowledge of where people both come from and go to, as well as lie in wait, namely, the soil. It is a demonstration of both a correct scientific understanding and, ironically, a biblical understanding as well, the Judaeo-Christian idea of "From dust to dust." It also reveals a moral imperative, a sense of moral responsibility to generations yet unborn.

The second story demonstrates a sophisticated knowledge of transpiration. Earth does indeed "breathe," in a manner of speaking, through its forests, a fact correctly identified by the Yanomami, undoubtedly a result of many centuries of living in this environment and a scientific observation and deduction through experience and focused observation rather than through what we would call "scientific method." If the world's forest is destroyed, the planet will have difficulty maintaining an atmospheric balance conducive to life on earth, analogous at least to the process of breathing (respiration) in animals or transpiration in plants. The cessation of either one leads to death.

These are only a few of many examples of a deep ecological understanding possessed by indigenous peoples, including Native Americans or Indians, revealing that these people have achieved both an understanding of and an accommodation with their environment, their ecosystem, similar to that which was likely achieved by our own European tribal indigenous forebears of centuries ago. Among modern peoples such an understanding has been lost or forgotten. And among the indigenous there is an accommodation to the ecological realities of the Americas, which we, as European-originated newcomers (in culture if not always in biology) have yet to achieve. Many spiritually based communities of sustainability often embrace native peoples' culture and wisdom on matters ecological, on matters pertaining to the land and ecosystems of North America.

Thus, the "science" as well as the spirituality of indigenous peoples becomes an important element in understanding such communities and their ecological approach. Eastern philosophy also enters into consideration with the thought, among others, of another Indian from a continent away, Vandana Shiva of India, a physicist by training and an agricultural scientist by practice, who holds to the philosophy, "There is Western science and there are other ways of knowing."[5] Western science refuses to accept this idea. In admitting that it cannot know or prove that there are no other ways of knowing, it reveals its own willingness and capacity to behave unscientifically when it so wishes. It claims to not itself be subject to the laws of nature. Western scientist Vandana Shiva thus opens the door for us to the legitimacy of non-Western science, including "Indian science," or "Native science," all of which have an ecological depth, appreciation, and sophistication which is not to be found in Cartesian-Newtonian mechanistic and reductionistic "Western science."

Thomas Berry's 1988 book, *Dream of the Earth*, contains a chapter on "The Historical Role of the American Indian." According to that chapter: "Religious personalities from the European culture have been especially limited in their ability to see the profoundly religious and spiritual qualities of the Indian traditions," qualities which have been strengthened by American tribal peoples' awareness "of having won a moral victory of unique dimensions during the past five centuries."[6] Berry's respect for tribal peoples' spiritual tradition is so great that he remarks that "they give to the human mode of being a unique expression that belongs among the great spiritual traditions of mankind."[7] He considers the Indians' spirituality a highly integral form in which the cosmic, human, and divine are present to one another in a way that is unique and that "This is precisely the mystique that is of utmost necessity at the present time to reorient the consciousness of the present occupants of the North American continent toward a reverence for the earth, so urgent if the biosystems of the continent are to survive."[8] Berry believes that, in some ultimate sense, we need their mythic capacity for relating to this continent more than they need our capacity for mechanistic exploitation of the continent.[9]

In his more recent book, *The Great Work*, Berry explains: "Their spiritual insight into the transhuman powers functioning throughout the natural world established the religions of Native Americans as among the most impressive spiritual traditions we know."[10] Faith-based communities of sustainability are open to and often reverent toward native peoples' ecologically grounded attitudes and often identify with aboriginal views of the natural order. Some might see them as respectful of the words of Chief Luther Standing Bear of the Lakota who has commented: "The white man does not understand America. He is too far removed from its formative processes. The roots of the tree of his life have not yet grasped the rock and soil. . . . But in the Indian the spirit of the land is still vested . . ."[11]

From the above we witness the obvious connectedness of sustainability, ecological values, spirituality, and indigenous peoples. We can also understand the value, therefore, of the contribution of the American indigene, actual and potential, to the subject of sustainability and spirituality, to the search for models of such value systems, and to an understanding as to why Thomas Berry, and other ecological writers and practitioners such as Sisters of Earth place such a high value on learning from the American Indian.

Perhaps the spiritually based ecological world view of the faith communities discussed in this volume is best captured in the words of Mabel Dodge Luhan of Taos, New Mexico, written many decades ago and recently republished:

I have never seen a look of anxiety, of exasperation over any kind of weather on an Indian face. Whatever comes in nature they meet it with acceptance as though it were right. They do not know how to resist natural things like drought or hail or cloudburst with anger and hate because they are so much at one with all the elements. They know they are themselves the earth and the rain and the sun, and when the sun sets they feel the peace and rightness of it. They watch the sun going down behind the horizon and they go down with it in a participation with its security and its gentle irrevocable progress that we have no experience of. We watch things happen in Nature as if they were outside us and separate from us but the Indians know they are that which they contemplate. . . . Natural weather just can't worry them, they have so much faith in Nature and in themselves. Will we ever recover our lost adjustment to this elemental life, or arrive at a new one so that we know everything is for the best in the best of worlds.[12]

In the indigene, science and spirituality clearly become one.

Preceding chapters have brought to the surface a great deal of social consequence, but have not focused directly on the question of justice, social, or ecological. The following chapter attempts to scratch the surface of that important subject.

Chapter Eight

SOCIAL JUSTICE MEETS ECO-JUSTICE

There is an increasing belief that peace without justice is an illusion. There is a further belief that justice for the Earth and justice for humanity require one another. Writing in a less esoteric and more pragmatic vein, Wes Jackson says, "Social justice has a better chance through the ecological door than through the industrial door, because the inputs are provided and don't have to be bought."[1] There is no denying that the question of social justice has been a traditional one for followers and practitioners of Judaeo-Christianity and of other faith beliefs as well.

Social justice is a central and fundamental component of ecological justice, and both forms of justice are taken as one and the same by the spiritually grounded practitioners of sustainability described in this volume. For some, a deep-seated feeling of social justice provides the entré into ecological spirituality and practice, while for others the two have always been inseparable as a single entity.

The broader question of eco-justice is a more recent arrival on the scene. Eco-justice, of course, encompasses both human and social justice but goes well beyond them, in time and in space. Some leading individuals and organizations in the field of social justice have been skeptical of, or even opposed to, eco-justice, or, at the minimum, have been uncomfortable with eco-justice and not fully certain what to make of it. They have suffered from a form of reductionism that has blinded them to the inherent connectedness of social or human justice as rooted in the broader totality of eco-justice. And the social eliteness of the environment movement in the United States has not been helpful in bridging the gap, creating that much more distrust in the minds of social justice workers and advocates. The gap, fortunately, is closing, and thus we are beginning to witness the activist involvement in eco-justice among some Catholic Bishops and their diocesan offices; among Protestant and Catholic ecumenical social justice organizations; and in other fora.

All of the individuals and communities described in this book see, or are coming to see, a direct correspondence between social justice and ecological well-being. They understand the interdependency between the struggle to liberate people and the movement to liberate the larger biosphere. And all of the women and men, religious and lay, Protestant and Catholic, mentioned in this chapter, would agree with Christian theologian Sallie McFague that the real sin of our age is the silent complicity of the churches and congregations in the impoverishment of others and the degradation of the planet.

This chapter's emphasis is not so much on definable communities per se as much as it is on looser communities of individuals working under institutional auspices to bring about a true marriage of social and eco-justice. A new community with much focus on broad questions of ecological sustainability can emerge from these efforts, communities which provide the networks and the seedbeds so necessary for the formation and sustenance of new communities of sustainability. New and broader more ecological definitions of sustainability can often result, as can the involvement of many people who might not otherwise become involved if the less traditional subject of eco-justice were required to stand alone.

HOUMA—THIBODAUX

A number of Roman Catholic Dioceses have something to teach in this area. The Diocese of Houma—Thibodaux in south Louisiana has been active in this domain for some two decades, far longer than most people would tend to think. This coastal region of south Louisiana, a land of swamps, bayous, and marshes rich with fish and seafood, is the home of Acadian (or Cajun) culture in the United States, the homeland of Evangeline, and of Cajun music and song. It is a region which has been vulnerable to and has suffered from serious problems of water quality degradation, coastal erosion and flooding, and serious negative experiences with the coastal fishing economy upon which so many local people depend.

It all started in the early 1980s with increasing denial of access to fishermen attempting to fish in their traditional area, a denial of access so serious that it led directly to an increase in demand from Church-run food pantries. That caught the attention of the local Bishop and his staff, notably Catholic Charities Director and Office of Social Justice Coordinator in the Diocese, Rob Gorman. Thus far, we are seeing a very traditional story. But one thing can lead to another and, if the spirit is open to nature, open to the Creation, as religionists might put it, things can move in other directions, including nontraditional directions such as the raising of ecological questions. (Severe coastal erosion and flooding, caused by denial of sediment replenishment into the Atchafalaya Delta, but also possibly exacerbated by sea level rise, water quality, air quality, energy conservation, and building (habitat) design and construction with recycled materials and serious energy conservation are all environmental matters in which the Catholic diocese is formally involved through the entré of social justice and its traditional social justice ministry and outreach.) There is also external involvement in these areas with the U.S. Catholic Conference, the National Association for Christianity, Religion and Ecology (NACRE), with the National Catholic Rural Life Conference, and with three other Catholic dioceses in Louisiana. Catholic churches are often used as the meeting locations for numerous kinds of environmental meetings. In addition, the diocesan youth program is focused on the Creation and on creation spirituality, and on ecological restoration projects as a critical element of Catholic teaching. Very traditional "boat blessings," or "blessing of the fishing fleet" services have now become focal points for creation spirituality. Applications for financial grants have been filed. There have been all-clergy, clergy, and lay meetings involving most of the priests and parish workers of the diocese, held at the Louisiana Marine Biological Laboratory in the coastal marshes, with focus on marine ecosystems, marine and fishery environmental questions, and inland in a state park, with focus on lands, forests, and wetlands questions. (A meeting of Catholic clergy on such questions and in these locations and for such purposes might come as a surprise to many.) (There is a Diocesean affordable housing program, not unusual in itself, but which is most unusual in the very high-energy efficiency and energy conservation component, an emphasis taken so seriously that six of these houses in the city of Houma have been recognized as the first four star energy-efficiency rated homes in the state of Louisiana.) There is also an accreditation system in the diocese for churches and congregations (which become known as "Protecting God's Creation Congregations"). Workshops on these subjects outside the diocese are conducted by diocesan personnel.[2]

The leadership of the Louisiana diocesan program is strong and deep, well established over two decades, and with good support from the Bishop. The thinking here is very open to the thought of Thomas Berry and what that represents. It is very attuned to legal structures and is able to engage opposition seriously and forcefully, and also well grounded in regional realities. Houma—Thibodaux could readily be a model for other Catholic dioceses, and for Christian churches and congregations more broadly; it clearly points to a spiritually based path to sustainability without necessarily the institutional infrastructure of most communities discussed in this volume.

AMARILLO

A second Catholic diocese which served as a seedbed for this approach to eco-justice is that of Amarillo in the Texas Panhandle. On the southern high plains, the Llano Estacado of legend, the Amarillo region is dominated by rolling short grass prairie, spectacular canyons, a strong Hispanic history and culture and, as well, a beef cattle/cowboy/ranching culture, and dry grass and irrigation agriculture. It is thus very different geographically, ecologically, and culturally from Houma—Thibodaux. It is also different in two other respects: the diocesan effort has actually led to a sustainability institution and community, albeit a very loose informal one, which is called the "Promised Land Network (PLN)." The effort has largely been spun off from the diocese, with the reality of the change in diocesan leadership to a Bishop with significantly less interest in such matters. But the roots in the diocese and the current participation level of clergy and laity from the diocese continue to link the project to the diocese, however broad and more ecumenical the project becomes. And the path into this ambitious West Texas project, spread over a ten thousand sq. mile region, clearly originated, like Houma—Thibodaux, from a base of traditional social justice concerns. In the Texas example, the group threatened was small-scale farmers, Hispanic in the "colonias" and Anglo across the region, and their needs were relative to land, livestock, habitat, and a secure economic existence. Eco-justice has come through the door opened by social justice. PLN (Promised Land Network) has also created and spun off a largely Hispanic organization, La CASA del Llano, which stands for "Communities Approaching Sustainability with Agroecology." La CASA is much more activist than PLN, leading some in the area to say that PLN talks and La CASA does.

The Promised Land Network, scattered across a vast area of the Texas Panhandle, is the brainchild of two Catholic priests of the Diocese of Amarillo and a lay employee of the diocese. Started as a land-based social justice project in this livestock and grain region of West Texas, the project set out to help small farmers being crushed by competition with industrial agriculture. (This includes very small-scale Hispanic land owners in the "colonias," poverty stricken communities reminiscent of Third World villages, but featuring land and small-scale livestock ownership, hence not without some potential for economic independence.) The teaching of English and the teaching of computer literacy, along with food security, have been cornerstones of the PLN effort, now largely carried out by La CASA. A major effort is being made by La CASA to partner with Heifer Project International (HPI) to do agro-ecology with both livestock and crops, to essentially use good principles of ecology and smallness of scale to improve the lives of very poor people and to give them economic independence. The original Catholic base of this project is becoming more broadly ecumenical and the project, although having an official status with the diocese, currently receives no support from the diocese due to a change in diocesan leadership. PLN itself is directly involved in community-building, education, and conference organizing, all focused on agro-ecology and spirituality; it sponsors a major conference in Amarillo or vicinity each winter. It is also involved in serious grass-fed natural beef production, some other livestock, large-scale composting of beef cattle waste into an economically (and ecologically) useable product, promotion of organic and low-input agriculture, biodiversity, and economic diversity, all strongly grounded in Christian social justice ministry.

This region of Texas is heavily dominated by beef cattle culture and by oil culture, which have, over time, developed "traditional" ways of doing things that are not questioned. These ways once worked, once fitted a niche, but no longer do, with great negative consequence to people and the ecosystem. Those who question become suspect. Thus, there is social pressure not to question. The result is great reticence to consider other alternatives, other ways of doing things. However, the composition of PLN and La CASA is strictly local and from old families who are highly regarded, partly offsetting defensive and antichange attitudes. All the leaders in these organizations are nature-based, very ecological in their thinking, and grounded with a very strong sense of place, in addition to their mature and strong spiritual commitment. They are visionary as well. An irony in this area is that West Texas was a mainstay of the early wind power industry, sponsored a form of agriculture which was strongly wind energy-dependent, and spawned and fostered a strongly independent-minded farm culture. Leadership of PLN comes out of this culture which was so dominant not so many years ago. [The farmers associated with PLN in this region of West Texas are certainly aware modern American farmers, but they appear to have a particularly strong ecological and spiritual value system (perhaps leading to a certain skepticism about the industrial agricultural model), a faith in the future, a clear vision of who they are, what they want to do, a sense of what they want for their children within the region (they clearly want them to remain there), and a very strong sense of place.] Additionally, through their religious belief, they have a strong sense of responsibility to the land, to their families and congregations, and to all among them who are less well off than they. They (and PLN) are guided by three questions:

- Where can we make room for family farming and ranching in rural and urban areas, for people of all races and socioeconomic conditions?;

- What structures and options are available to enhance and empower the lives of men, women, and children on farms, ranches, and in local communities?;

- How should current roles of men, women, and children be strengthened, challenged, and restructured to build a fuller participation in a sustainable agriculture?.

These are questions which are not being asked within the current culture dominated by oil and industrial agriculture.

PLN's core effort in answer to these questions is to teach about biointensive methods of producing food in order to build local sufficiency and empowerment. It is a faith-based incubator of ideas and resources for ecological sustainability and social change, and is itself a community of networkers. Additional to the above, PLN has been actively involved in microenterprise to assist small businesses (through La CASA), and in the purchase, renovation and use of an historic building (Home Mercantile in Nazareth, Texas), used for public and community cultural and other kinds of events and celebrations which build and strengthen the PLN and its region. It also publishes a quarterly newsletter (now discontinued) and sponsors radio spot programs, sponsors agro-ecological farm tours, and rural faith formation nights. PLN refers to itself as a values-based network gathering people and collaborating in creative ways to educate and advocate for sustainable agriculture and communities.

PLN has been challenged by the reality of its regional location and threatened by a big farm and agri-business cattle culture which is not sympathetic, and, as well, by a significant change in church leadership in the Diocese. It is also challenged by geographic realities (vast distances), and by the often countervailing responsibilities of its leaders. It has survived, but it remains to be seen if it has an ability to last beyond the time of its founders. Nevertheless, it does provide a strong model of a spiritually based and ecologically based sustainability project and network (or community), in part because it recognizes there can be no ecological sustainability without cultural sustainability. It exemplifies what such a group can accomplish in terms of helping to inculcate a deep ethic of sustainability in those people whose lives it touches.[3]

LAS CRUCES

Southern New Mexico lies at the northern edge of the Chihuahuan Desert, a region of temperature extremes, a land of aridity and treeless mountains bisected by the agriculturally fertile but narrow Rio Grande Valley. Like Amarillo, it is a land of Hispanic culture, albeit with less Anglo presence. Here in the Catholic Diocese of Las Cruces activist Bishop Ricardo Ramirez, has perhaps given us the clearest example in the nation of social justice become eco-justice, for the Diocese and its many projects represent a true seamless garment when it comes to its borderless approach to both. And the diocesan staff actually conducting these projects are a powerful arm of a determined Bishop. Las Cruces Diocese has converted traditional social justice projects in the colonias, in aid of the poor, the oppressed, the discriminated against, the unemployed, the least powerful among us, with a highly enlightened approach to ecology and environment. The Rio Grande, the river and its riparian ecosystem, and its ecological health, is analogous to and related to the people it supports.

In an interview, Bishop Ramirez spoke of the enormous amount of life in the Rio Grande in spite of the great pollution load and destruction. The river just keeps giving life in spite of it all, the Bishop says, and he sees an analogy here to people, people who always have the capacity to, as he says, give life. But where, Bishop Ramirez asks, are the Hispanic voices contributing to the environmental/ecological discussion and witness? Perhaps their history of marginalization and oppression has stifled their ability or their inclination to speak out, to witness, in this way.[4]

The Diocesan concern over the condition of the colonias, not the least their environmental circumstance, and, as well, the lost opportunity they represent, as recognized by PLN in Texas, is certainly very much in the mind of diocesan workers and activists. Equally so the plight of small-scale Rio GrandeValley farmers and farm workers. The Diocese is also active in environmental issues, including directly in the recently defeated siting of a proposed medical waste incinerator in Sunland Park near the Mexican border, and a privately owned and operated industrial landfill in the same community, both directly fought by the Bishop. The Diocese, displaying its enlightenment and progressive nature, would clearly rather put its energy into building things, and things that last, rather than stopping or preventing things (though it is not naïve in recognizing that both works are often necessary). In this building process, community organizing and mutual support community building are both necessary, and diocesan efforts in this work are organized by a highly skilled and experienced community organizer, Antonio Lujan.[5]

Earlier in this volume, I described the extremely successful collaboration of the Diocese with Franciscan Sisters and Sisters of Charity to establish the eco-community of Tierra Madre, at forty-seven houses the largest strawbale housing development in the United States. At the other end of the Diocese, in Silver City, can be found another major diocesan economic development and eco-development project equally as formidable in effort, the Grant County Cooperative Development Project.[6] This three parish—supported and diocesan—supported project, influenced by the very successful Mondragon Industrial Model of worker-owned cooperatives in Spain, is essentially a wood pellet/wood chip production cooperative. Economic slowdown and high unemployment in the copper mine—based Silver City area from the national economic recession of the late 1980s led the Diocese to develop a project not only to create employment so as to reduce the impact of the recession on many local families, but also to begin the process of creating true economic independence for these people. Regional economic diversification also results, as does focused assistance on the poorest of the poor, very much in keeping with the stated social justice mission of the Catholic Church and of Catholic social teaching.

This project also involves direct cooperation with the neighboring Gila National Forest and its U.S. Forest Service staff. Thinning operations for fire control in this very large national forest yield excess thin logs which have no traditional market (because of small diameter), but which can be used in the production of nonconventional (but actually highly traditional in New Mexico) latias and vigas (thin log roofing) and bark products for horticulture, landscaping and erosion control/ground cover, and ultimately to wood pellet manufacture. Tierra Alta Fuels, a private nonprofit, has been established by the Diocese, and spun off by the Diocese, for this purpose.

This work is not without some environmental concerns. Most agree on the timber cutting for fire control and timber stand improvement (with fire retardation in the driver's seat throughout the West today), but some environmentalists argue that downed small diameter timber should remain on the land to return nutrient to the soil. Other environmentalists, however, work with the cooperative, both because of its social justice values and also because the wood pellets produced displace dependency on fossil fuel, creating a useable fuel which represents both recycling and an optimal renewable alternative energy resource, both important environmental objectives.

Community-based forestry is the ultimate goal here. Sawdust, dried chips, and wood pellets are the three products produced. The Mescalero Apache Indian Reservation is one of a few other sources for raw material.

The Silver City District Ranger on the Gila National Forest is enthusiastic about the future prospects for this collaboration, as the Forest Service is planning a 1,200 acre ponderosa pine restoration in a ponderosa pine stand, which is sprinkled with a small amount of Emery, Gray, and Gambel's oak understory. There have been no commercial timber sales in this area for almost two decades and grazing was terminated a few years ago. Thus, thinning for fire control is becoming very important and any demand that can be created for the product, even from a nonprofit, is desirable from the Forest Service perspective. The demonstration of this as an urban interface project is also important to the Forest Service.

Remarkably, the small diameter ponderosa pine of these thinnings has the same Btu (British thermal unit) (energy) value as hardwood oak, since there is no wood density issue when it comes to pellets. And, as long as the tree diameter does not exceed nine inches, the cuttings can be given away rather than sold (as required of a sawlog, i.e., a log more than nine inches in diameter) under federal law. The process is from logs to chips to sawdust to reconstitution as wood pellets. Essentially, the Diocese of Las Cruces has provided, in cash and in kind $60,000 per year for five years, which further secured another $100,000 in state capital grant outlay. There are some additional donors.

What has happened in my experience here is that a Bishop, through his assistant, has led me to a U.S. Forest Service District Ranger, and on to an industrial cooperative—a chain of events which could never have happened a decade or more ago. This is indicative of a changed culture at the religion—natural resources—environmental conservation interface, and may well portend things to come.

The subject of worker-owned industrial cooperatives (vis-à-vis Mondragon in Spain) and workplace democracy combined with Catholic social teaching and an option for the poor and downtrodden constitutes the philosophical underpinning of this whole project. This philosophy, combined with very high quality and highly committed leadership, has insured a story to tell at Silver City and in the Diocese of Las Cruces. The Diocese, of course, is key, yet the project (and others like it) has been spun off from the diocese in order to insure its long-term continuation (and to preclude any damage which might result from change of leadership at the diocesan level, should that occur). The only weak aspect of this project currently is the difficulty of getting raw material. And the project must find a way to be competitive as a nonprofit up against for-profit enterprises. Sound business acumen of its staff leadership is most helpful here.

In sum, among Tierra Madre, Tierra Alta Fuels, and numerous small environmental and agricultural examples, I know of no greater example than the Catholic Diocese of Las Cruces to illustrate in its action the marriage of the option for the poor (the traditional approach) and the option for the Earth (the new broader agenda), for in Las Cruces they are truly one.

Activism in Las Cruces can also be found at the individual parish level; it is not limited to the diocesan hierarchy. There has been a combination in some churches of antiwar and peace activism with an emerging and deep interest in environment and ecology, an eco-activism. This suggests that, not only in New Mexico but around the country, there are a number of priests who are tired of traditional and limited parish work and who are anxious to bring out their deep and very often life-long interest in Nature. They want to work to protect Nature as their priestly ministry.

HEIFER PROJECT INTERNATIONAL (HPI)

Heifer Project International (HPI), an ecumenical and interdenominational Christian organization with strong support from Methodist, Presbyterian, and UCC churches, also with Catholic and other Christian involvement, grew out of the Christian social call to feed the hungry. Started in the immediate aftermath of post-World War II destruction and loss of food supply for Europeans, its work has now spread worldwide, including within the United States. The idea is simple: private contributors enable HPI to provide a milk cow or other livestock to a hungry family, in return for a commitment to breed the animal and donate the first offspring to some other needy family, the gift that keeps giving as it's been called. Today, most HPI activity is in the Third World nations of Asia, Africa, and Latin America, and "livestock" is defined as any live animal which can provide food sustainability and economic security to a needy family and which can be bred and passed along. This could include camels, water buffalo, rabbits, honeybees, numerous types of fowl, as well as all standard farm animals, including beasts of burden.

Headquartered in Arkansas, HPI maintains a large ranch where for years many animals were raised and bred for shipment overseas. Today, most animals are bred in the region of their ultimate destination so the HPI ranch today is more of a learning and demonstration center and a center for materials distribution than a ranch. During its extensive work over many decades, HPI has had to learn to live with the realities and considerable constraints of Third World villages and rural areas. This has forced an ecological approach, and this is where traditional Christian social justice ministry meets the much newer Christian eco-justice ministry. Sustainability of these families, as well as that of the HPI program, requires adherence to more eco-centric thinking. The famous and much used "Third World Village," a kind of generic and typical Latin American, African, and Asian simulated Third World village constructed in the Arkansas hills at the HPI ranch, built for training and demonstration purposes, has turned out as well to be an excellent tool for the education of Americans, Americans seeking to understand the Third World reality, yes, but Americans who will also get a good dose of ecology as part of that understanding. Thus, HPI came to ecology and sustainability not directly through their Christianity, but through the back door, in a manner of speaking, via human social concern and the encounter with Third World necessity.

It was perhaps inevitable at HPI that livestock breeding would ultimately be broadened to include crops for food and fiber as well, and agro-ecology and sustainable agriculture, including the techniques of permaculture, are now a lively and probably permanent part of the practice and discourse at HPI.

HPI's headquarters are in the city of Little Rock, and a new education/demonstration Third World village will be constructed at a high profile site in that city, undoubtedly one which will bring more attention to HPI's move toward matters ecological. But the work at the ranch in the hills west of Little Rock continues apace, and the ranch, being a living/learning institution, is also itself a community with ecological obligations. Does it practice what it preaches, therefore, is a legitimate question it must face. And does it do so both in terms of what ecology requires, and also in terms of its interpretation of Christianity?

In recent years the HPI ranch has undergone a change from a true ranch breeding livestock (and teaching and demonstration) to a largely educational facility, and much of its considerable acreage has been leased out for local cattle production. No other livestock is any longer bred at the site, although a few camels, water buffalo, donkeys, sheep, hogs, guinea fowl, cattle, and draft horses are kept for show purposes and to maintain tradition. There is now on the site some new emphasis on crops and gardens, on a new organic garden of some size, an active CSA project, seed-saving and heirloom variety breeding, a greenhouse, herb production, intensive raised bed gardens, and a permanent horticulturist on staff, all indicative of HPI's move away from strictly livestock tradition to agro-ecology. Present also are now more aggressive agricultural sustainability ideas, some holistic resource management practice with cattle, some pasture chicken projects, and educational and character-building activities, the latter a somewhat new thrust.

Although HPI's work has been primarily focused on helping those in need elsewhere, there is direct application of the ecological principles in practical use there to the United States. In addition, HPI itself has a small but growing domestic United States effort focused on low-income families and regions, but not without value to the nation at large. HPI has the means and the status to become a major player in the area of agriculturally oriented ecological sustainability in the United States, if it chooses to do so, and, as well, to do this as part of its interpretation of the requirements of Christian faith. Its small farm initiatives and the high level of economic and ecological sustainability associated with them can be transformative to many people and can send a powerful message to the society at large. And, at the ranch itself, a community of sustainability is being established. The community has strong ecological philosophy, with staff inspired by Wendell Berry, E. F. Schumacher (small is beautiful—appropriate technology), David Orr, Aldo Leopold, Thomas Berry, and other important ecological thinkers, although not without practical challenge in its own operations and the need to bring others not so ecologically educated along in these directions. HPI will suffer the challenge, as do all of us, to walk our talk, and will undoubtedly be watched in its own building design, energy consumption and sources, food sources, and other daily behavior, and its national credibility will be related to how the organization itself conducts its affairs, at the ranch and in Little Rock.

There is a substantial amount of community sustainability being practiced at HPI's ranch, and serious effort is being made toward ecological sustainability. With an exceptionally good use of volunteers, with energy conservation, with recycling, with organic food production (and with the food used in their own cafeteria), one finds that HPI practices what it preaches.[7]

GHOST RANCH

The Presbyterian educational and retreat center known as Ghost Ranch in New Mexico bears a few similarities in its circumstance to that of Heifer Project International. Also a Christian ecumenically based center for experiential education, and increasingly for demonstration, Ghost Ranch is specifically Presbyterian in its Christian approach and ownership. It is a twenty-one thousand acre working ranch, located in the stunningly beautiful high desert mountain and red rock canyon country of northern New Mexico so recognizable through the painting of American Southwest painter Georgia O'Keefe. But the ranch is also moving more to demonstration in its livestock activity (in contrast to food production). The ranch hosts continuing year-round educational and character development programs, and some religious programs, many with a strong eco-spiritual bent. These include some number of weeklong and multiweek workshops directly on eco-spirituality. Ghost Ranch has also been an important sustainable agriculture demonstration center (production of heirloom varieties, new ecological breeds for high altitude deserts, holistic resource management practice, demonstration gardens, food purchasing policies favoring small local farmers, organic growers, etc.), and is a growing center for ecological design, solar energy, strawbale housing, and even strawbale offices, and so forth. There is a formidable library of regional ecological and eco-spiritual materials, and an especially important bookshop of such subjects, which demonstrates the strong interest of visitors and staff in ecological and spiritually grounded sustainability philosophies. There is also a major wetlands development project which handles all of the ranch's sewage disposal, a community farm supplying some food to the institutional kitchen (though less than in the past), and a good recycling program for disposal but not for purchasing of recycled product. Except for a small amount of solar energy and the energy conservation values of the few strawbale buildings, most energy is drawn from an unsustainable source, highly polluting coal-fired power plants.

The Presbyterian Church USA has a strong record of interest in and involvement in social justice. And Presbyterianism's contemporary interest in eco-spirituality has been strong. So, it is natural that the Ghost Ranch bookshop and library should be strong in those areas, in the theological area of immanence more than transcendence, and in an appreciation of a strong sense of place (and in regional American Indian cultures as part of that sense of place). It is also natural that a strong start would have been made on the ground in ecological agriculture, in alternative energy source, in building design, in food purchasing policy, and so forth, and in attention to these subjects in the visitors and educational program which can involve five hundred resident participants on site for a week at a time. There is a strong suggestion here of a positive ecological conscience and at least a past willingness to respond tangibly to contemporary concern.

Ghost Ranch is also, however, a model of the challenge of how to sustain ecological values over time and through changing circumstances and leadership. At the ranch, there is a direct connection made very often between the requirements and moral teaching of Christianity (Presbyterianism in particular), and our response to the destruction of the Creation. And yet, reversals of some ecological initiatives (community gardens, food purchase policy, limitations on ecological building design, reliance on coal, lack of composting, link of certain measures strictly to saving money, or perhaps image, rather than dictate of faith belief, and a general lack of food or energy policy, a tangible drifting governed by price), all significantly reduce the opportunity of Ghost Ranch to show spiritually based leadership in these directions. And the retrogression of Ghost Ranch in the past decade could worsen when one or two key leaders in ecological directions are ultimately replaced. Ghost Ranch is a model for the challenge of how to keep sustainability projects themselves sustainable, and to do so in a culture which resists. Ghost Ranch with its enormous potential presents a significant opportunity to authentically model ecological values within the framework of contemporary Christianity.[8]

OTHER EXAMPLES

Other "social justice to eco-justice" examples may be drawn from spiritually directed but totally nonsectarian projects ranging from non-governmental community cooperatives and organizations to occasionally public entities like the state cooperative extension services which sometimes sponsor programs assisting and working closely with small-scale growers, with women in agriculture (i.e., women-owned enterprises), and minority-owned enterprises. Because these categories of persons are viewed as disadvantaged and left out or not served by the mainstream, and because they are sometimes congregated in specific areas, they can constitute communities of sustainability of sorts, and can demonstrate implicitly a strong spiritual drive which is not explicit on the surface (and which, if a public entity, cannot be present explicitly).

Within this category I would place the much written about Ganados del Valle small-scale economic development cooperative in northern New Mexico. This is small-scale private enterprise, land and livestock based (sheep and wool, woven goods, local foods), which is involved in and celebratory of regional history and Hispanic culture. This example represents rootedness in and a sense of place, community values, appreciation of small scales, with a high priority on local employment and empowerment of local people; implicit spirituality based on eight generations on the land; and rooted in implicit ecological principle.

There are other such efforts around the nation (though few could claim a heritage of eight generations!)

The work of the New Mexico Center for Sustainable Agriculture is part of the state Cooperative Extension Service and is active in only a few counties of northern New Mexico. It is indicative of a small-scale social justice—economic empowerment—ecologically based project—and, I would argue, with a strong sense of spirituality grounded within the culture (Hispanic, and, to some extent, Indian). This program is involved in local farmers markets, recognizing the crucial importance of marketing to keep people on the land and to keep small-scale sustainable agriculture sustainable. And many grazing associations have been started through the Center as well, as have "grass banks" to provide for future quality grazing opportunity for the small ranchers. Food processors are next on the agenda. The leadership of the Sustainable Agriculture Center also reminds us that you can't have ecological sustainability without cultural sustainablility, that ecological sustainability must be grounded in an ethic acceptable to the long-term cultural heritage of the people, or it cannot succeed. Herein lies an important element of the spirituality which lies just beneath the surface of this public project.

Northern New Mexico microscale agricultural activities are reminiscent of similar New England microscale agricultural enterprise. The response of government (Cooperative Extension Service) to this small size is not only a reflection of reality, but also is motivated in New Mexico by Hispanic and Indian agricultural and cultural realities, and the political need to respond to them. Less obvious is a direct cultural or spiritual question, or one of oppression, in New England, except perhaps spirituality of the "back-to-the-land" movement. A similar situation to New Mexico's exists in the deep-South with the effort, although quite insufficient, to assist and sustain African-American farmers.

An interdenominational social justice—eco-justice effort, organized and run by the New Mexico Council of Churches and participated in by a number of Protestant denominations and all three Catholic dioceses in the state is a group called "Stewards of Creation." (Chaired by activist and the long-time Executive Director of the New Mexico Council of Churches, Wallace Ford, and funded by foundation grants as well as churches, Stewards of Creation is a serious experiential, educational project, statewide, to give members of church congregations and parishes the tools to lead their own local faith communities very strongly in the direction of eco-justice, and significantly from a human or social justice root.) Grounded solidly in the philosophical and cosmological work of Thomas Berry and Brian Swimme, this program promotes both theory and practice in moral and ethical discernment through Christian (Protestant and Catholic) faith belief, and in ecological sustainability.

The purpose of this effort is that faith communities statewide should become themselves centers of earth stewardship through project-based learning, through spiritual motivation, through revaluing the Earth, and through vocational formation, significantly to be achieved through an understanding and application of Thomas Berry's work. In the first year, twenty persons became a learning community, meeting twelve times in twelve different locations around the state engaging with twelve different issues, and for a period of two days and two nights in each meeting. These meetings, covering all regions of the state of New Mexico, ranged in subject matter from climate change, urban sprawl, land use, air and water pollution, water rights and wilderness, to farming, ranching, mining, and more regionally oriented Native American environmental issues and international border issues.

Some of the twenty participants will become trainers for similar learning and advocacy communities in their own churches and for subsequent groups of twenty new stewards each year in a continuing replication of the program. The idea of Stewards of Creation is to move beyond environmentalism to social justice issues about which Christianity requires moral concern, and it builds on the foundational vocation which all Christians are called upon to share as part of their baptismal experience.

Stewards of Creation explicitly puts itself forth as a response to Thomas Berry's book, *The Great Work*, and thus shares directly in a philosophical way with the Sisters of Earth communities. It is also explicitly grounded in social justice, equates social and eco-justice, and is thus properly situated with other spiritually grounded sustainability efforts described elsewhere in this chapter, albeit of the networking rather than the institutional category. A model here has been developed, one which is wholistic, complete and effective. There is no reason it cannot be replicated in many other places.[9]

The Center for Action and Contemplation, a Franciscan (Catholic) institution in Albuquerque, New Mexico, is a living example of the strong, passionate, deeply rooted social justice philosophy of ecologically inspired Franciscan friar Richard Rohr. This philosophy, expressed through many books and tapes over long years, implicitly supports eco-logical justice through its insistence on the structural and institutional components of social justice, as well as its exceedingly strong critique of consumption and consumerism. As the Center's name implies, the strength of the proecological, anticonsumeristic activism derives from strong respect for the necessity of contemplation, and the need for the two to work in tandem. In other words, contemplation must lead to activism, which in turn must lead to contemplation, which must lead to activism, in an endless cycle. The physical operation of CAC facilities, including its retreat center, "Tepeyac," is a study in ecological perfection (food, energy, waste disposal, daily cycles of life, library, etc.), grounded in some of the most passionate and yet pragmatic spiritually grounded social philosophy to be found anywhere. The Center's quarterly newspaper, *Radical Grace*, clearly suggests, by name and content, the radical nature of both Christianity and ecology, as both are seen by this Center and its nationwide network.[10]

Richard Rohr would undoubtedly agree with the Las Vegas, New Mexico based philosopher and practitioner of ecological sustainable agri-culture, Mark Feedman. Feedman, the former director of the Luna Voca-tional-Technical Institute's practical agriculture programs (and of other such sustainable agriculture programs around the country), and an archi-tect of many hands-on applied agricultural sustainability projects with major social justice and empowerment ramification says: "Sustainability and consumerism are diametrically opposed to one another; thus, sus-tainability and capitalism are opposed. That is why people do not want to think about or talk about true sustainability!" Further, "Distortion of terms (including sustainability) is used to favor the status quo, to avoid change, and to avoid questioning the value system."[11] Feedman points out that the sustainable agriculture movement was and is a farmers move-ment, and that very few people are actual practitioners of sustainability, and therefore finding people who can do it is very difficult. Reflecting on higher education, Feedman says that the people associated with the sus-tainable agriculture movement are not only telling the university they no longer have a place, but that they've done wrong. Feedman's long career in New Mexico, in the Dominican Republic, and in other places has been dedicated to rectifying that. The centerpiece of his effort has been his Sus-tainable Rural Development Program, his own creation, a program which focuses upon the highest agricultural yield from a limited resource base (even involving triple digging and employment of traditional Indian agriculturally sustainable methods, and not far from the challenge facing Heifer Project International). His approach is to work with nature, rather than changing it through genetic engineering or controlling it through pesticides, herbicides, and artificial fertilizers. "If we kill all the bugs, the bad ones will come back, but the good bugs won't—the real damage will be done,"[12] Feedman says.

Two more purely sustainable agriculture efforts, both nongovernmental, which bear the mark of social justice through eco-justice (and rooted more in ecological than in social justice), and both, I believe, spiritually driven implicitly (though not at all explicitly) are the Kerr Center for Sustainable Agriculture in Oklahoma, and Wes Jackson's Land Institute in Kansas. Kerr operates a four thousand acre project in eastern Oklahoma oriented toward creating a community of sustainable agriculture practitioners statewide in Oklahoma. Formerly deeply involved in on-site experimentation and demonstration of livestock and crop sustainability, from holistic resource or ecological management for beef cattle to pasture hogs, pasture chickens, sheep, and other livestock and organic crop fields, Kerr has now moved more toward crops (especially berries, wine grapes, heirloom varieties of vegetables), paralleling HPI's move from all livestock concentration to a much greater openness to crops and agro-ecology. And Kerr has also moved much more out into the state with its producer grants program, the current centerpiece of its efforts. It is also heavily focused on direct marketing for farmers and is the primary mover for farmers markets and establishment of a farmers market alliance for Oklahoma. Their Center is now a "stewardship ranch," as they refer to it, and their expressed mission is to aid the transition to organic agriculture, to locally grown food, and to direct marketing. They want to help sustain present organic growers and encourage others to convert, offering support for the transition. They are aided in this process in Oklahoma by U.S. EPA's removal from the market of many chemicals. The farmers had been dependent on these chemicals and find their replacement difficult, impossible or very expensive, and thus face reduced choices. This situation has made them more open to looking at, appraising and even adopting organic methods. Culturally, the conversion to organic has not been easy in Oklahoma, as farmers who do so can be rejected and isolated, and that is where Kerr comes in. When these farmers approach the Kerr Center, besides receiving "how to" information, they are matched up with a farmer-mentor from their area of the state who is currently farming organically. The Center is also developing Oklahoma-based manuals for small-scale and organic producers (which suggests an inadequacy of support for these farmers by the Cooperative Extension Service), and, as well, is developing training manuals for market managers of farmers markets. Kerr Center also seeks to influence public policy in these subject areas and maintains a staff in the state capitol. Organic certification (including for bees), holistic resource management, farmers markets, and direct producer grants are the essence of Kerr's work. A strong newsletter and many substantial technical publications are produced by the Kerr Center, in addition to the training manuals and a number of sociological surveys. The writings of Wendell Berry are a strong philosophical underpinning.

Kerr is building a network of sustainable community, land- and farm-based, with great application to small-scale and other underserved farm populations. It stands foursquare for eco-justice and social justice, and is implicitly if not explicitly spiritually inspired.[13]

Wes Jackson and his Land Institute at Salina in central Kansas, and his model sustainability town at Matfield Green in southeast Kansas, provides some parallels to the Kerr Center. Agriculturally and scientifically based, governed by a strong philosophical foundation of ecological sustainability (I would argue spiritually inspired and on Christian precepts), and with social justice ramifications and roots, the Land Institute program is gathering a region-wide (not restricted to Kansas) and even nationwide following; the Institute is influencing a whole generation of Americans who know of this project and support it toward land and food systems sustainability. Jackson and his books and articles are powerful in the national food and sustainability dialogue, and he and his organization have received much international recognition for their work, work which is foundational to the national effort in ecological sustainability. Once again, one finds the two Berrys, Wendell and Thomas, and David Orr and others as deep sources of inspiration to Jackson and the Land Institute, who themselves are instructive and inspirational to so many others.[14]

All of these constitute living examples of social justice broadening itself to eco-justice, predicated upon spiritually grounded ecological principles.

If, by this point, connectedness has been established between spirituality and sustainability, as incomplete as that effort could be in this small volume, how might we respond?

Chapter Nine

CONCLUSION

I have forever believed that two great forces power existence, from the insect world to the world of human beings. The first is the force that compels us to live, to endure, to procreate, to strive for all the things that sustain us in a living state. The second force is the one that connects us to all other animals and plants. The life force empowers every living creature to fight for life. The connective force is a gentler drive that makes every creature respond to the other creatures with which it shares the world. It is the force that bows our heads and makes us all embrace the fact that we are only a small part in the enormous matrix of life. As human beings we are quite aware of the life force. But with our unique, imperfect, cognitive powers, we have developed institutions that mute the connective force. While industrialization, specialization, capitalism, and religions scream the mantra of Life, Life, Life, they also whisper a tacit denial that we are connected significantly to the rest of the planet. Such human institutions ignore the inevitability of life cycles, mortality and humility. They explode the balance of life. Without the connective force we are left with only one force to guide our lives: Life, Life, Life at all costs."[1]
—Dan O'Brien, *Buffalo For the Broken Heart:
Restoring Life to a Black Hills Ranch*

The Sisters of Earth, the monks, other Christian religious, lay and clerical, indigenous peoples, and others mentioned in the preceding chapters are undoubtedly gentle but forceful and determined connectors. Through their words, yes, but even much more strongly and clearly through their deeds and their practice, they would qualify in rancher Dan O'Brien's words as primary exemplars of the connective force.

It is an unstated but very implicit premise throughout this book that actions speak louder than words. "The proof is in the pudding" goes an old cliché. Of course, words and actions, action and contemplation, must work in a continuous circle and must recycle with one another. Both are important. Both are necessary. But we must also accept that we live in a society, the early-twenty-first-century American society, which has a severe imbalance, a surfeit of words, and a scarcity of actions. Thus, the lesson we must learn is the need for balance, and an understanding of the seminal importance of practice, of action. Our values are in the way we behave, and behave daily. They are not necessarily in our words and, indeed, may be far removed from, even opposite to, our word. Giving lip service to ecology and its principles, while refusing to live in or practice an even remotely ecological lifestyle, gets us nowhere and even threatens to reduce our own self-respect. The people described in this book, while facing all the same challenges we all face in our modern world, have learned how to resist, and they stand as models for all of us of how to significantly overcome those challenges, to indeed live ecologically. The resistance they demonstrate, the rejection of antiecological and thus destructive behavior, can be difficult but is central. And it is best achieved not through negative acts but through positive acts, as demonstrated in so many different ways in this book.

The preceding chapters have also made clear the need for rectification of another imbalance, this on the spiritual side. That is the need, particularly in Christian spirituality, to balance immanence and transcendence, as our forebears once did until perhaps five or six hundred years ago. To recognize the Creator in the Creation, the sacrality of all, is a lost philosophy and practice which must be resurrected if we are to have any hope of resolving our problems of sustainability. We must recognize the permission to abuse and destroy which has come out of the multicentury deification of transcendence, of God separate and above, removed from the scene, of a "sky God" in theologian Sallie McFague's term. We have failed in modern times to recognize or respect the revelatory aspect of nature (that there are two books of revelation, as Tom Berry and others have told us, Scripture and Nature), and thus the need for reverence (far more than respect) in our dealing with Nature, Nature as us, for, as ecology teaches, we are one. Without this balance of immanence (God or the sacred in all) and transcendence (God or mystery above and beyond, beyond our ability to conceptualize or understand), there will be no hope for the children, neither humanity's future generations, nor the children of all species.

It has been stated both implicitly and explicitly in this book that true or real sustainability, in contrast to cosmetic or shallow sustainability, requires something much more than simply doing things in a new way, of achieving greater efficiency, of saving money, of a desire to be kind to nature, and so forth. Given that the real thing, that is, real sustainability, is countercultural to our fossil fuel-based, high energy and consumption-addictive, and high speed society, it takes far more than simplistic notions to resist the seduction, conditioning, and pressure of that society. And yet that resistance is necessary to open the path for alternative behavior. The mainstream society is fundamentally not only ecologically insensitive but far worse, it is ecologically averse. It is determinedly antiecological, often so in its rhetoric, but most always in its action, in its behavior. Far more is necessary to overcome such an obstacle. Spirituality, deeply held spiritual belief, religion, religious faith, however we might define these things, are all necessary to achieve real sustainability. That has been the premise running throughout this volume. Thus, the study of spiritually inspired and faith-based models of sustainability grounded literally and figuratively in the soil and in faith, is valuable and is the very justification for this book.

Sustainability and Spirituality presents the reader with a slice of this experience across several regions of the United States. There is no attempt here at comprehensiveness—undoubtedly readers will be able to point out other examples in other places which have gone unmentioned in this text, and are perhaps even unknown to me. But what the reader has encountered in this volume is breadth of geography, breadth of ecological circumstances, and breadth of examples of ways of living and emphases within faith-based communities of ecological sustainability, largely within the Christian cultural and theological tradition, that tradition which is of dominant influence (regardless of one's personal religious belief) within the American society.

Interestingly, many of the case examples described in this book are in states and regions not known for ecological or environmental identity. It is perhaps appropriate to look now to a possible future case study, one located in the northeastern United States and within a state which does have a reputation for identity with ecological and environmental thought and movements: Vermont.

Along a rural road high up in the Green Mountains of central Vermont can be found a roadside sign that reads "Green Mountain Monastery." Behind that sign lies a few hundred acres of pasture, field, and woodland, unbuilt-upon and returning to natural forest long after farming ended here. Where is the monastery? One is invited to also ask the question, What is a monastery? Is the sign premature? Is the sign telling us that this is the future site of a monastery? No! The sign claims, and is meant to claim, that this is a monastery. For the record, a new monastic community is planning to locate itself on this site, some buildings are planned, some of the land will be returned to agriculture to feed the community, and so forth. But the community, monastic religious women of the Catholic Passionist order, would argue that the land, the ecosystem, is itself the monastery, just as will be the buildings, the chapel, the farmland, and so forth, when they are developed. The Creation is sacred, they would say, no less than the chapel and other buildings. They are not here arguing for nature worship, for the worship of Nature as divine—that would be pantheism—but rather reverence for Nature as sacred, available for our reverence, not our abuse. And Nature to them, as to any ecologically literate person, is inclusive of humanity—there is no duality.

Planned for this mountain pasture site in Vermont is the world's first "Ecozoic Monastery," literally monastery for the "Ecozoic Age," to use Tom Berry's terminology. Thomas Berry himself, also a Passionist monk and Catholic priest, is the incorporator of this monastery along with Sr. Gail Worcelo and Bernadette Bostwick, Passionists who have come from St. Gabriel's Monastery in Pennsylvania at the invitation of the Catholic Bishop of the Diocese of Burlington (Vermont) to establish a new monastic community. Berry often writes of the Ecozoic Era, the age of evolution into which we are transitioning, he says, as we leave the Cenozoic Era or Age of the present and recent past. Berry sees the Ecozoic as an Age of Ecology in which ecological principle will govern. An "ecozoic monastery," therefore, is one which will take very seriously and will seriously practice ecological principles, and will do so in the context of its spirituality, its faith belief, its charism, within the model of monasticism human society has developed and which this book has discussed.

A picture of this monastic community at Green Mountain Monastery five or so years down the road should bear some similarity to the sustainability models presented in chapter three, "Outstanding Models of Sustainability." It would be a blend also with chapter six on "Monasticism, Sustainability and Ecology," and with chapter four, on Thomas Berry and his thought, while reflecting Sisters of Earth of chapter five in the very formal choice of name of this new monastic foundation or community. The principles of land stewardship, of diversified sustainable agriculture, of habitat and building construction and design, of energy conservation and alternative energy, and of behavioral practices such as purchasing, waste disposal, transportation, and related areas of everyday life should clearly reflect much of the preceding in this book. Likewise, the liturgy, based in Catholic Christianity but highly ecumenical, and interested in ecological and spiritual tenets of non-Western peoples (indigenous people, Eastern philosophies) and hence universal in the true catholic (as well as Catholic) sense, will reflect the sacrality of Creation and creation spirituality so fully subscribed to by the many communities represented in this book. And all will be conducted in the monastic style brought to this place by the founders.[2]

Actions do speak louder than words, and it is the models revealed in this book, not the theory, which will be our true teachers and which, therefore, represent the highest value of this work, work which fittingly represents Thomas Berry's "Great Work." The people described in this book are all engaged in that "Great Work."

NOTES

_____

CHAPTER ONE: INTRODUCTION

1. Steven C. Rockefeller, "The Earth Charter: Building a Global Culture of Peace," in *The Ecozoic Reader* 2, no. 1 (fall, 2001): 8.

2. The Sisters of Earth communities and the monastic examples described in this volume are Catholic, but they are clearly infused with indigenous peoples' spirituality (i.e., Native American) and, to some extent, Eastern religions and philosophy. More importantly, all the examples are exceedingly ecumenical in nature and, in truth, the Sisters and the monastic communities are visited by and supported by more Protestants, agnostics and other non-Catholics than they are by Catholics. They are, therefore, representative of something much broader than Catholicism. And, since non-Catholic denominations don't as often have religious orders, men's or women's, and don't as often form religious communities, such examples as these are less frequently encountered outside of Catholicism.

CHAPTER TWO: ON SUSTAINABILITY, RELIGION, AND ECOLOGY

1. As delineated and described by environmental scientist Barry Commoner in his book *The Closing Circle: Nature, Man and Technology* (New York: Knopf, 1971). See especially pp. 33–46.

2. Aldo Leopold, *A Sand County Almanac and Sketches Here and There* (New York: Oxford University Press, 1949).

3. On sustainability of the collectivity, of the community, Wendell Berry writes that, "(I)f the members of a local community want their community to cohere, to flourish, and to last, these are some things they would do:

(1) Always ask of any proposed change or innovation: What will this do to our community? How will this affect our common wealth?

(2) Always include local nature—the land, the water, the air, the native creatures—within the membership of the community.

(3) Always ask how local needs might be supplied from local sources, including the mutual help of neighbors.

(4) Always supply local needs first. (And only then think of exporting their products, first to nearby cities, and then to others.)

(5) Understand the unsoundness of the industrial doctrine of "labor saving" if that implies poor work, unemployment, or any kind of pollution or contamination.

(6) Develop properly scaled value-adding industries for local products to insure that the community does not become merely a colony of the national or global economy.

(7) Develop small-scale industries and businesses to support the local farm and/or forest economy.

(8) Strive to produce as much of the community's own energy as possible.

(9) Strive to increase earnings (in whatever form) within the community and decrease expenditures outside the community.

(10) Make sure that money paid into the local economy circulates within the community for as long as possible before it is paid out.

(11) Make the community able to invest in itself by maintaining its properties, keeping itself clean (without dirtying some other place), caring for its old people, teaching its children.

(12) See that the old and the young take care of one another. The young must learn from the old, not necessarily and not always in school. There must be no institutionalized "child care" and "homes for the aged." The community knows and remembers itself by the association of old and young.

(13) Account for costs now conventionally hidden or "externalized." Whenever possible, these costs must be debited against monetary income.

(14) Look into the possible uses of local currency, community funded loan programs, systems of barter, and the like.

(15) Always be aware of the economic value of neighborly acts. In our time the costs of living are greatly increased by the loss of neighborhoods, leaving people to face their calamities alone.

(16) A rural community should always be acquainted with, and complexly connected with, community minded people in nearby towns and cities.

(17) A sustainable rural economy will be dependent on urban consumers loyal to local products. Therefore, we are talking about an economy that will always be more cooperative than competitive." Wendell Berry, *Another Turn of the Crank* (Washington, D.C.: Counterpoint Books, 1995), pp. 19–20.

4. Revealing some of their underlying philosophy, the Nearings have written:

The Guiding Principles begin with the affirmation of the interconnectedness of existence, the overarching relatedness of all aspects of life. In embracing a context of relations—of theory and practice, nature and culture, the human and nonhuman, mind and body, labor and leisure, intellect and spirit, knowledge and morals—the separate principles of the Good Life are in themselves part of the web of life woven of all the principles together.

One's sense of wholeness emerges from daily routines, allowing for study, reflection and meditation. The good life affords opportunity to provide for physical needs as simply and in as few hours as possible so that remaining time and energy is devoted to the search for truth and consideration of its sacred source. Cultivating the spirit is not only equal in importance to cultivating one's garden, but its radiance is reflected in the rows and furrow, in the seedlings and harvest. The harvest is the wonder and enchantment of the world.

In periods of silence and solitude the individual can confront their true self, make contact with the larger aspects of life and reach toward a cosmic consciousness. Solitude inspires critical self-reflection to question the assumptions that hold our world together. Reflection unveils the awareness of incongruity between what one espouses and what one does, providing motivation for personal and social transformation.

The art of self-communion has died before the dread of self-revelation. To sit at rest under a shady tree; to wander alone for hours through the woods and under the stars; to paddle out over the shadowy depths of the lake, alone; to contemplate, and enjoy,—These are phases of life little known because they imply that dreadful task of facing things as they are and that still more awful necessity of facing things as they may be and will be. Men and women cling to their companions in order that their worst fears may not be realized.

Men dread isolation; they seek madly to pile up this world's goods, and rushing into the market-place, they crowd close among their companions, their souls crying aloud for succor and encouragement. After years of such a life, they awake to the presence of an isolation more frightful than any other which the world can conceive—the isolation of the individual in a crowd, the marooning of a human soul on the island of goods which it has heaped together.

The road to isolation lies through a struggle for supremacy in which dead things are the insignia of success. He who would draw himself near to his neighbor must first bear his own soul to himself.

Live within your income; spend less than you get; pay as you go.

When the time comes that men believe in themselves rather than in the things they possess, a long stride will have been taken toward the reduction of the denominator of wants. So long as men believe in salvation through the possession of goods, so long they will continue to suffer." Helen and Scott Nearing, *Guiding Principles for a Good Life* (Harborside, Maine: The Good Life Center, 1997), p–1.

CHAPTER THREE: OUTSTANDING MODELS OF SUSTAINABILITY

1. Sacred Heart Monastery can be reached at P.O. Box 364, Richardton, North Dakota 58652. Web address is *www.rc.net/richardton*.

2. Sr. Paula Larson, O.S.B., interview by the author, Sacred Heart Monastery, Richardton, North Dakota, August 2000.

3. Sr. Bernadette Bodine, O.S.B., "Benedictines and the Wind on the Prairies," Sacred Heart Monastery Website, 2000.

4. Sr. Paula Larson, O.S.B., "North Dakota Winds Become Rich Blessings for Us," Sacred Heart Monastery Website, 2000.

5. Ibid.

6. Tierra Madre can be reached at 115 Mesa Verde, Box 1768, Sunland Park, New Mexico 88063.

7. Permaculture is defined as a set of design principles which can be used to develop sustainable systems to meet human needs simultaneously, for food, shelter, and energy. Its core principles include:

- thoughtful observance of natural systems and consciously designed environments which mimic the patterns and relationships found in nature;
- full recycling of energy and nutrient needs on the farm or within the community;
- use of local resources over external ones;
- utilization of each element (plant, animal, structure, etc.) in all of its functions, rather than treating each as separate elements;
- design for relative location and connection of related elements to provide the most efficient beneficial interchanges of functions and needs;
- sharing what we learn with others.

8. Heartland Farm can be reached at R.R. #1, Box 37, Pawnee Rock, Kansas 67567.

9. Prairiewoods can be reached at 368 Forest Drive S.E., Cedar Rapids, Iowa 52403.

10. Michaela Farm can be reached at P.O. Box 100, Oldenburg, Indiana 47036.

11. Sr. Ann Marie Quinn, O.F.M., interview by author, Michaela Farm, March, 2000.

12. Michaela Farm Mission Statement, 1995.

13. Michaela Farm Mission Statement, 1999.

CHAPTER FOUR: THEORY BEHIND THE PRACTICE

1. Thomas Berry and Thomas Clark, S.J. *Befriending the Earth: A Theology Reconciliation Between Humans and the Earth* (Mystic, Connecticut: Twenty-Third Publications, 1991), p. 9. Tom Berry is not to be considered a "guru" so much as an articulator of a certain body of thought, highly ecologically based, which is in use in many of these communities, including in places not directly familiar with his work.

2. Ibid., p. 97.

3. Thomas Berry, interview by author. Weston, Vermont, October 2001.

4. Thomas Berry, *The Great Work: Our Way into the Future* (New York: Bell Tower Books, 1999), p. 77.

5. Sr. Miriam Therese MacGillis, O.P., *To Know the Place for the First Time: Explorations in Thomas Berry's New Cosmology* (Sonoma, California: Global Perspectives, 1991), (set of six audio-cassette tapes).

CHAPTER FIVE: WE WILL NOT SAVE WHAT WE DO NOT LOVE

1. Statement from the Fourth International Conference of the Sisters of Earth, Santa Barbara, California, August 2000. Some of the women religious involved in these communities view their effort as very modest, only a beginning, and themselves as latecomers to this work. I agree with this assessment, but believe such modesty underestimates the movement's potency, and its ability to bring congruence to spiritually based, faith-based sustainability. In time we will come to see the power of this congruence to affect change.

2. Yushi Nomura, trans., *Desert Wisdom: Sayings from the Desert Fathers* (Maryknoll, New York: Orbis Books, 1982), p. 108.

3. Written at the invitation of the Council (in Rome) of the General Superiors of Women's Religious Communities in a longer form entitled "Religious Women as the Voice of the Earth."

4. Thomas Berry, *Religious Women as the Voice of the Earth*, n.p., unpublished.

5. Ibid.

6. Ibid.

7. Ibid.

8. Ibid.

9. The phrase "Sisters of Earth communities" commonly used on these pages, refers to those communities of women religious and allied lay women who have centrally committed themselves to live their charism on the land and conduct their behavior within the basic principles of ecology ("earth principles," as it were).

10. Dante, Alighieri. *The Divine Comedy*. Edited and translated by Robert M. Durling (New York: Oxford University Press, 1996).

11. Sr. Gail Worcelo, C.P., interview by the author, Weston, Vermont, October 19, 2002.

12. Fourth International Conference, August 2000.

13. For a full definition of "permaculture," see chapter three, endnote 7.

14. St. Mary-of-the-Woods Earth Literacy Graduate Program may be reached at the College of St. Mary-of-the-Woods, which has its own post office and zip code at Saint Mary-of-the-Woods, Indiana 47876–1089.

15. The White Violet Center for Eco-Justice may be reached at Sisters of Providence, St. Mary-of-the-Woods, Indiana 47876–1089.

16. The Marianist Environmental Education Center can be reached at Mt. St. John/Bergamo, 4435 East Patterson Road, Dayton, Ohio 45430–1095.

17. Villa Maria can be reached at EverGreen, P.O. Box 206, Villa Maria, Pennsylvania 16155.

18. The SSND Center for Earth Spirituality and Rural Ministry can be reached at 170 Good Counsel Drive, Mankato, Minnesota 56001–3138.

19. The Churches Center for Land and People can be reached at General Delivery, Sinsinawa, Wisconsin 53824–9999.

20. The Sisters of St. Joseph of Nazareth Center for Ecology and Spirituality, may be reached at 3629 Gull Road, #3, Kalamazoo, Michigan 49001.

21. The Dominican Earth Project may be reached at Office of Earth Education and Sustainable Living, Dominicans of St. Catherine Kentucky, 2645 Bardstown Road, St. Catherine, Kentucky 40061–9435.

22. "A Ten Year Plan for Earth Care," St. Catherine Dominican Motherhouse, St. Catherine, Kentucky, 1999, p. 1.

23. Genesis Farm may be reached at 41A Silver Lake Road, Blairstown, New Jersey 07825.

24. Albert Fritsch, S.J., personal correspondence on August 10, 2002. Al posits ten elements in his treatment of eco-spirituality:

(1) *Authenticity:* All authentic eco-spiritualities enrich us. In order to be authentic these should be respectful of others, compassionate especially for the poor, and open to spiritual growth and development.

(2) *Respect:* The spirituality must be willing to recognize the power of the Creator, embrace the Earth, and learn to be in close harmony to the rhythms of all of creation. Through the use of our mental powers we recognize our place on this planet and so we gain a deeper understanding of natural phenomena in our lives.

(3) *Compassion:* An eco-spirituality must be aware of the poor (people and other creatures) and be willing to suffer with them so that they may take or retain their rightful place in the total environment. Our compassion springs from our heart and includes an urgency to overcome the vast divide between the "Haves" and the "Have-nots" of this Earth.

(4) *Openness:* A spirituality that is totally self-contained is simply out of touch with the movement of history. Through our head and heart proceeds the work of our hands, the great manifestation of the Spirit within. We are committed to assist in building a New Earth, and we invite others to join in this noble enterprise.

(5) *Plurality:* All authentic spiritualities have an ecological content. Part of spreading the Good News is to assist adherents of a variety of spiritualities to find and affirm their contributions to building the New Earth. Variety is ecologically healthy.

(6) *Eco-Feminism:* Women have a unique contribution to the healing of the Earth, and they do not have to take the lead of male thinkers or gurus to reveal these gifts.

(7) *Rest:* All people should have the right to free time and periods of silence and relaxation wherein prayerful reflection may occur. In our

stressful and rushing society, little space is given to individuals to practice their own spirituality.

(8) *Discernment:* Authenticity also has a counterpart which is spiritual movements which are not enriching. One must discern the good from the bad, using centuries-old widely accepted spiritual exercises. Some spiritualities are demeaning.

(9) *Religion:* Eco-spirituality should enhance religious practice and not stifle it in any way. All are expected to be faithful to their religious traditions and see that the affirmation of ecological values within these will improve the spiritual environment of all people.

(10) *Critique:* All spiritualities are subject to critique so that growth may continue to occur.

25. Albert Fritsch, S.J., *Reflections on Land Stewardship* (Mt. Vernon, Kentucky: Appalachia—Center for Science in the Public Interest, 2001). Al's claim that the greatest environmental problem facing the religious communities in America is the demise of the largest amount of undeveloped land holdings in urban America is a subject that could well constitute a whole other book.

26. The National Catholic Rural Life Conference (NCRLC) can be reached at 4625 Beaver Avenue, Des Moines, Iowa 50310–2199. Their website is *www.ncrlc.com*. NCRLC's 1996 publication, *Religious Congregations on the Land: The Practical Links Between Community, Sustainable Land Use, and Spiritual Charism* (48 pages) is one of the few texts extant on this subject.

27. From a commencement address of Winona LaDuke at Antioch College, Yellow Springs, Ohio, April 28, 2001.

28. *Proceedings of the Land Stewardship Conference for Religious Communities at Milford, Ohio* (Mt. Vernon, Kentucky: ASPI Publications, 2000), p. 92.

29. National Catholic Rural Life Conference (NCRLC), *Religious Congregations on the Land*, p. 3.

30. U.S. Catholic Conference, *Renewing the Earth: An Invitation to Reflection on the Environment in Light of Catholic Social Teaching* (Washington, D.C.: U.S. Catholic Conference, 1991), p. 2.

CHAPTER SIX: MONASTICISM, SUSTAINABILITY, AND ECOLOGY

1. Nomura, trans., *Desert Wisdom*, p. 68.

2. Dr. Albert Fritsch, S.J., *Environmental Assessment Report for Osage Monastery* (Sand Springs, Oklahoma: Osage Monastery, 1994), p. 1.

3. Theodore Roszak, *Person/Planet* (Garden City, New York: Anchor Press/Doubleday, 1979).

4. Roszak, *Person/Planet*, p. 285.

5. Ibid., p. 287.

6. Ibid., p. 289.

7. Ibid., p. 294.

8. Ibid.

9. Roszak, *Person/Planet*, p. 295.

10. Ibid., p. 301.

11. Ibid., p. 303.

12. Morris Berman, *The Twilight of American Culture* (New York: W. W. Norton and Co., 2000), pp. 135–136.

13. Ibid., p. 157.

14. Kathleen Norris, *Cloister Walk* (New York: Riverhead Books, 1996), p. 63.

15. Ibid., p. 92.

16. Ibid.

17. Thomas Berry, interview with the author, Weston, Vermont, October 2, 2002.

18. Thomas Merton, *The Wisdom of the Desert: Sayings from the Desert Fathers of the Fourth Century* (New York: New Directions, 1960), p. 3. Merton also writes of the "hidden wholeness" that is to be found in all visible things, further enhancing his credibility as an ecological thinker. Parker Palmer, contemporary writer on spirituality, further expands on what he calls the "paradox" of this "hidden wholeness" in that it holds together in plain sight life and death, light and darkness, beauty and diminishment, which are not opposites when seen in the context of this hidden wholeness.

19. Ibid., p. 9.

20. Thomas Merton, *Mystics and Zen Masters* (New York: Farrar, Strauss and Giroux, 1967), p. 18. Other useful Thomas Merton books include *Conjectures of a Guilty Bystander* (1965), and *Zen and the Birds of Appetite* (1968).

21. Ibid.

22. Thomas Merton, *The Wisdom of the Desert*, pp. 22–23.

23. Fr. Romuald, O.S.B., Camal., interview with the author. April 1996.

24. Br. Benet Tvedten, O.S.B., *The View from a Monastery* (New York: Riverhead Books, 1999), p. 11.

25. Ibid., p. 53.

26. Ibid., p. 121.

27. Terrence Kardong, O.S.B., "Ecological Resources in the Benedictine Rule," in Albert LaChance and John E. Carroll, *Embracing Earth: Catholic Approaches to Ecology* (Maryknoll, New York: Orbis Books, 1994), p. 167.

28. Ibid., p. 168.

29. Ibid.

30. Ibid.

31. Ibid., p. 144.

32. Ibid., p. 145.

33. Hugh Feiss, O.S.B., "Watch the Crows," in *And God Saw That it Was Good: Catholic Theology and the Environment* (Washington, D.C.: U.S. Catholic Conference, 1996), p. 151.

34. Ibid., P. 152.

35. Ibid.

36. Ibid., p. 162.

37. Sr. Joan Chittister, O.S.B., *Wisdom Distilled from the Daily: Living the Rule of St. Benedict Today* (New York: Harper/Collins, 1991), p. 168. See also by Joan Chittister, O.S.B., *The Rule of Benedict: Insights for the Ages* (New York: Crossroads, 1996).

38. Ibid., p. 169.

39. Ibid., p. 170.

40. Ibid., p. 174.

41. Ibid., p. 176.

42. Ibid., p. 177.

43. Ibid., p. 178.

44. Ibid., p. 179.

45. Ibid., pp. 179–180.

46. Ibid., p. 180.

47. See Robert Craig, "Learning from Each Other: Benedictine and Native American Perspectives on the Environment," paper presented at the Benedictine Perspectives on the Environment Conference, Atchison, Kansas, 1997.

48. Larry Rasmussen, *Earth Community/Earth Ethics* (Maryknoll, New York: Orbis Books, 1996), p. 134.

49. Russell Butkus, "Sustainability and the Benedictine Way: An Eco-Theological Analysis," at Benedictine conference Perspectives, p. 6.

50. Ibid., pp. 29–30.

51. Richard Bresnahan, "Indigenous Realization of Community: Clay Work and Worship, Shared Sensibility as a Common Rural Background of Benedictine Environment," at Benedictine conference, Perspectives. Bresnahan also writes that Wendell Berry's seventeen principles of community sustainability are a contemporary clarification of the Rule of Benedict for use both inside and outside of monastery walls.

52. Ibid., p. 10.

53. John Klassen, O.S.B., "The Benedictine Vow of Stability and Environmental Stewardship," at Benedictine Perspectives conference, p. 5.

54. Ibid., p. 7.

55. Ibid.

56. Hugh Feiss, O.S.B., "Water, Oneness and the West: Benedictine Theological Reflections," at Benedictine Perspectives conference.

57. Sr. Phyllis Plantenberg, O.S.B., interview with the author, College of Saint Benedict, St. Joseph, Minnesota, July 2000.

58. John Klassen, O.S.B., interview with the author, Saint John's University, Collegeville, Minnesota, August 2000.

59. Assumption Abbey is in Richardton, North Dakota.

60. Osage Monastery can be reached at 18701 W. Monastery Road, Sand Springs, Oklahoma 74063, and on the web at *www.benedictinesisters.org*. For background on Christian monasticism, particularly Benedictine (the most prominent form), see *Benedictines*, a semi-annual journal published at Mount St. Scholastica Monastery, Atchison, Kansas 66002. See also the *American Benedictine Review*, published at Assumption Abbey in Richardton, North Dakota, and *Tjurunga*, the Australasian Benedictine journal.

61. Albert Fritsch, S.J., *Environmental Assessment Report for Osage Monastery.*

62. The Monastery of St. Benedict is located at 17825 South Western Street in Canyon, Texas 79015.

63. The Monastery of Christ in the Desert can be reached at 1305 F.S. Road 151, P.O. Box 270, Abiquiu, New Mexico 87510–0270.

64. The Cistercian Abbey of Our Lady of the Mississippi is located on the Mississippi River near St. Donatus, Iowa.

65. New Melleray Cistercian (Trappist) Monastery is located just southwest of Dubuque, Iowa.

CHAPTER SEVEN: ON SCIENCE

1. Reductionism is the belief that truth is to be found in the parts, in reducing, dividing, isolating the whole. It stems from Cartesian, Newtonian, Baconian thinking (after René Descartes, Sir Isaac Newton, and Francis Bacon), and remains dominant in mainstream thought, though not without challenges. It is sometimes called "Cartesian" or "mechanistic thought." Reductionism, the tendency to reduce and divide in an attempt to understand, is contrary to the first principle of ecology, the idea that everything is interconnected with, interdependent with, dependent upon everything else for its being, its essence, its reality, and that all exists in relationship. Ecology, and all the communities described in this book, are philosophically counter to reductionism, and critical of it, implicitly and sometimes explicitly.

2. Terrence Kardong, O.S.B., "Elements of Process Thinking in the Rule of Benedict," *Tjurunga: An Australasian Benedictine Review* 54 (May 1998): 6.

3. David Bohm's findings and work are best described in his book *Wholeness and the Implicate Order* (London and Boston: Routledge and Keegan Paul, 1980).

4. Langdon Gilkey, *Nature, Reality and the Sacred: The Nexus of Science and Religion* (Minneapolis: Fortress Press, 1993).

5. Vandana Shiva is the author of many books on this subject, including *Staying Alive: Women, Ecology and Development* (1989); *The Violence of the Green Revolution: Third World Agriculture, Ecology and Politics* (1991); *Biopiracy* (1999); *Stolen Harvest* (2000); and *Tomorrow's Diversity* (2001), among others.

6. Thomas Berry, *Dream of the Earth* (San Francisco: Sierra Club Books, 1988), p. 183.

7. Ibid., pp. 182–183.

8. Ibid., p. 184.

9. Ibid., p. 190.

10. Thomas Berry, *The Great Work: Our Way into the Future* (New York: Bell Tower, 1999), p. 37.

11. Luther Standing Bear, *Land of the Spotted Eagle* (Boston: Houghton-Mifflin, 1933), p. 248.

12. Mabel Dodge Luhan, *Winter in Taos* (Albuquerque, New Mexico: Horizon Communications, 1982), pp. 195–196.

CHAPTER EIGHT: SOCIAL JUSTICE MEETS ECO-JUSTICE

1. Wes Jackson, interview with author, The Land Institute, Salina, Kansas, April 4, 2001.
2. The Diocese of Houma—Thibodaux Office of Social Justice is at 1220 Aycock, Box 3894, Houma, Louisiana 70361.
3. The Promised Land Network (PLN) can be reached at P.O. Box 1844, Hereford, Texas 79045–1844. La Casa del Llano is at 309 East 6th Street, Hereford, Texas 79045.
4. Bishop Ricardo Ramirez, interview with the author, Las Cruces, New Mexico, February 2000.
5. The Diocese of Las Cruces Social Justice Office is at 1280 Med Park Drive, Las Cruces, New Mexico 88005.
6. The Grant County Cooperative Development Project can be reached through county offices in Silver City, New Mexico.
7. Heifer Project International (HPI)—Heifer Ranch can be reached at Rt. 2, Box 33M, Perryville, Arkansas 72126.
8. Ghost Ranch is at HC 77, Box 11, Abiquiu, New Mexico 87510.
9. Stewards of Creation can be reached at 8302 San Juan NE, Albuquerque, New Mexico 87108.
10. The Center for Action and Contemplation (CAC) can be reached at 562 Atrisco SW, Box 12464, Albuquerque, New Mexico 87195-2464.
11. Mark Feedman, interview with the author, Las Vegas, New Mexico, March 18, 2001.
12. Ibid.
13. The Kerr Center for Sustainable Agriculture can be reached at P.O. Box 588, Poteau, Oklahoma 74953.
14. The Land Institute is at 2440 East Water Well Road, Salina, Kansas 67401.

CHAPTER NINE: CONCLUSION

1. Dan O'Brien, *Buffalo for the Broken Heart: Restoring Life to a Black Hills Ranch* (New York: Random House, 2001), p. 245.
2. Sr. Gail Worcelo, C.P., "An Ecozoic Monastery: Sharing a Transforming Vision for the Future," in *Loretto Earth Network News* (spring 2000): 7. The monastery, still under development, may be reached at 38 River Road, North Chittenden, Vermont 05763.

BIBLIOGRAPHY

Badiner, Allan Hunt. *Dharma Gaia: A Harvest of Essays in Buddhism and Ecology*. Berkeley: Parallax Press, 1990.

Barnhill, David, and Roger S. Gottlieb. *Deep Ecology and World Religions*. Albany: State University of New York Press, 2001.

Berman, Morris. *The Twilight of American Culture*. New York: W. W. Norton and Co., 2000.

Berry, Thomas, C.P., with Thomas Clarke, S.J. *Befriending The Earth: A Theology Of Reconciliation Between Humans And The Earth*. Mystic, CT: Twenty-Third Publications, 1991.

Berry, Thomas. *The Dream of the Earth*. San Francisco: Sierra Club Books, 1988.

Berry, Thomas. *The Great Work: Our Way into the Future*. New York: Bell Tower, 1999.

Berry, Wendell. *Another Turn of the Crank*. Washington, D.C.: Counterpoint Books, 1995.

Boff, Leonardo. *Ecology and Liberation: A New Paradigm*. Maryknoll, New York: Orbis Books, 1995.

Bohm, David. *Wholeness and the Implicate Order*. London and Boston: Routledge and Kegan Paul, 1980.

Bresnahan, Richard. "Indigenous Realization of Community: Clay Work and Worship, Shared Sensibility as a Common Rural Background of Benedictine Environment." Benedictine Perspectives Environment Conference. Atchison, Kansas: n.p., 1997.

Brockelman, Paul. *Cosmology and Creation: The Spiritual Significance of Contemporary Cosmology*. Oxford, England: Oxford University Press, 1999.

Butkus, Russell. "Sustainability and the Benedictine Way: An Eco-Theological Analysis." In Benedictine Perspectives Environment Conference. Atchison, Kansas: n.p., 1997.

Capra, Fritjof, and David Steindl-Rast. *Belonging to the Universe*. San Francisco: Harper/Collins, 1991.

Carroll, John E., and Keith Warner, O.F.M. *Ecology and Religion: Scientists Speak*. Quincy, IL: Franciscan Press, 1998.

Carroll, John E., Paul Brockelman, and Mary Westfall. *The Greening of Faith: God, the Environment and the Good Life*. Hanover, NH: University Press of New England, 1997.

Chittister, Joan Sr. O.S.B. *Wisdom Distilled from the Daily: Living the Rule of St. Benedict Today*. New York: Harper/Collins, 1991.

———. *The Rule of Benedict: Insights for the Ages*. New York: Crossroads, 1992.

Christiansen, Drew, S.J., and Walter Grazer. *And God Saw That it Was Good: Catholic Theology and the Environment*. Washington, D.C.: United States Catholic Conference, 1996.

Cobb, John B., Jr. *Is it Too Late? A Theology of Ecology*. Beverly Hills, CA: Bruce, 1972.

Commoner, Barry. *The Closing Circle: Nature, Man and Technology*. New York: Knopf, 1971.

Cummings, Charles, O.C.S.O. *Eco-Spirituality: Toward a Reverent Life*. New York: Paulist Press, 1991.

Craig, Robert. "Learning from Each Other: Benedictine and Native American Perspectives on the Environment. In Benedictine Perspectives Environment Conference. Atchison, Kansas: n.p., 1997.

Dalton, Anne Marie. *A Theology for the Earth*. Ottawa: University of Ottawa Press, 1999.

DeWitt, Calvin B., ed. *The Environment and the Christian*. Grand Rapids, MI: Baker Book House, 1991.

DeWitt, Calvin B. *Caring for Creation*. Grand Rapids, MI: Baker Book House, 1998.

Edwards, Denis. *Jesus the Wisdom of God: An Ecological Theology*. Maryknoll, New York: Orbis Books, 1995.

Evans, Bernard F., and Gregory D. Cusack, eds. *Theology of the Land*. Collegeville, MN: The Liturgical Press, 1987.

Feiss, Hugh, O.S.B. "Watch the Crows." In *And God Saw That It was Good: Catholic Theology and the Environment*. Washington, D.C.: U.S. Catholic Conference, 1996.

Feiss, Hugh Fr, O.S.B. "Water, Oneness and the West: Benedictine Theological Reflections." In Benedictine Perspectives Environment Conference. Atchison, Kansas: n.p., 1997.

Fox, Matthew. *Original Blessing*. Santa Fe, NM: Bear and Company, 1983.

Fragomeni, Richard N., and John T. Pawlikowski, O.S.M., eds. *The Ecological Challenge: Ethical, Liturgical and Spiritual Responses*. Collegeville, MN: The Liturgical Press, 1994.

Fritsch, Albert J., S.J. *Down to Earth Spirituality*. Kansas City, KS: Sheed and Ward, 1992.

———. *Reflections on Land Stewardship*. Mt. Vernon, Kentucky: Appalachia—Center for Science in the Public Interest, 2001.

———. *Renew the Face of the Earth*. Chicago: Loyola University Press, 1987.

————. *Enviromental Assessment Report for Osage Monastery*. Sand Springs, Oklahoma: n.p., 1994.

Gilkey, Langdon. *Nature, Reality and the Sacred: The Nexus of Science and Religion*. Minneapolis, MN: Fortree Press, 1993.

Gottlieb, Roger S., ed. *This Sacred Earth: Religion, Nature, Environment*. New York and London: Routledge and Kegan Paul, 1996.

Hallman, David G., ed. *Ecotheology: Voices from South and North*. Maryknoll, New York: Orbis Books, 1994.

Hamilton, Lawrence S., ed. *Ethics, Religion and Biodiversity: Relations Between Conservation and Cultural Values*. Cambridge, England: The White Horse Press, 1993.

Haught, John F. *The Promise of Nature: Ecology and Cosmic Purpose*. New York: Paulist Press, 1993.

Hill, Brennan R. *Christian Faith and the Environment: Making Vital Connections*. Maryknoll, New York: Orbis Books, 1998.

Kardong, Terrence, O.S.B. "Ecological Resources in the Benedictine Rule." In *Embracing Earth: Catholic Approaches to Ecology*. By Albert LaChance and John E. Carroll. Maryknoll, New York: Orbis Books, 1995.

————. "Elements of Process Thinking in the Rule of Benedict." *Tjurunga: An Australasian Benedictine Review* 54 (May 1998):6.

Kaza, Stephanie. *The Attentive Heart: Conversations with Trees*. New York: Fawcett Columbine, 1993.

Kellert, Stephen R., and Timothy J. Farnham, eds. *The Good in Nature and Humanity: Connecting Science, Religion, and Spirituality with the Natural World*. Washington, D.C.: Island Press, 2002.

Klassen, John, O.S.B. "The Benedictine Vow of Stability and Environmental Stewardship." In Benedictine Perspective Environment Conference. Atchison, Kansas: n.p., 1997.

LaChance, Albert, and John E. Carroll. *Embracing Earth: Catholic Approaches to Ecology*. Maryknoll, New York: Orbis Books, 1994.

Leopold, Aldo. *A Sand County Almanac and Sketches Here and There*. New York: Oxford University Press, 1949.

Lonergan, Anne, and Caroline Richards. *Thomas Berry and the New Cosmology*. Mystic, CT: Twenty-Third Publications, 1988.

Luhan, Mabel Dodge. *Winter in Taos*. Albuquerque, NM: Horizon Communications, 1982.

MacGillis, Sr. Miriam Therese, O.P. *To Know the Place for the First Time: Explorations in Thomas Berry's New Cosmology*. Sonoma, CA: Global Perspectives, 1991.

McDaniel, Jay B. *Earth, Sky, Gods and Mortals: Developing an Ecological Spirituality*. Mystic, CT: Twenty-Third Publications, 1990.

McDaniel, Jay B. *Of God and Pelicans: A Theology of Reverence for Life*. Louisville, KY: Westminster, 1989.

McDaniel, Jay B. *With Roots and Wings: Christianity in an Age of Ecology and Dialogue*. Maryknoll, New York: Orbis Books, 1995.

McDonagh, Sean. *Passion for the Earth: The Christian Vocation to Promote Justice, Peace and the Integrity of Creation.* Maryknoll, New York: Orbis Books, 1994.

McDonagh, Sean. *The Greening of the Church.* Maryknoll, New York: Orbis Books, 1990.

———. *To Care for the Earth: A Call for a New Theology.* London: Geoffrey Chapman, 1986.

Merton, Thomas. *The Wisdom of the Desert: Sayings from the Desert Fathers of the Fourth Century.* New York: New Directions, 1960.

———. *Mystics and Zen Masters.* New York: Farrar, Strauss, and Giroux, 1967.

Nasr, Seyyed Hossein. *Religion and the Order of Nature.* Oxford, England: Oxford University Press, 1996.

Nearing, Helen and Scott. *Guiding Principles for a Good Life.* Harborside, Maine: The Good Life Center, 1997.

Nomura, Yushi, trans. *Desert Wisdom: Sayings from the Desert Fathers.* Maryknoll, New York: Orbis Books, 1982.

Norris, Kathleen. *Cloister Walk.* New York: Riverhead Books, 1996.

Northcott, Michael S. *The Environment and Christian Ethics.* Cambridge, England: Cambridge University Press, 1996.

O'Brien, Dan. *Buffalo for the Broken Heart: Restoring Life to a Black Hills Ranch.* New York: Random House, 2001.

Oelschlaeger, Max. *Caring for Creation: An Ecumenical Approach to the Environmental Crisis.* New Haven, CT: Yale University Press, 1994.

Rae, Eleanor. *Women, the Earth, the Divine.* Maryknoll, New York: Orbis Books, 1994.

Rasmussen, Larry. *Earth Community/Earth Ethics.* Maryknoll, New York: Orbis Books, 1996.

Roberts, Elizabeth, and Elias Amidon. *Earth Prayers from Around the World.* San Francisco: Harper/Collins, 1991.

Rockefeller, Steven C. "The Earth Charter: Building a Global Culture of Peace." In *The Ecozoic Reader* 2, No. 1 (fall, 2001):8.

Rockefeller, Steven C., and John C. Elder, eds. *Spirit and Nature: Why the Environment is a Religious Issue.* Boston: Beacon Press, 1992.

———. *The Ecozoic Reader* 2, No. 1 (Fall, 2001):8.

Roszak, Theodore. *Person/Planet.* Garden City, New York: Anchor Press/Doubleday, 1979.

Santmire, H. Paul. *The Travail of Nature.* Minneapolis, MN: Fortress Press, 1985.

Scharper, Stephen Bede. *Redeeming the Time: A Political Theology of the Environment.* New York: Continuum, 1997.

Scharper, Stephen Bede, and Hilary Cunningham. *The Green Bible.* Maryknoll, New York: Orbis Books, 1993.

Sheldrake, Rupert. *The Rebirth of Nature: The Greening of Science and God.* New York: Bantam Books, 1991.

Snyder, Gary. *The Practice of the Wild.* New York: North Point Press, 1990.

Snyder, Gary. *A Place in Space: Ethics, Aesthetics and Watersheds.* Washington,
    D.C.: Counterpoint, 1995.
Standing Bear, Luther. *Land of the Spotted Eagle.* Boston: Houghton-Mifflin,
    1933.
Swimme, Brian. *The Hidden Heart of the Cosmos.* Maryknoll, New York: Orbis
    Books, 1996.
————. *The Universe is a Green Dragon.* Santa Fe, NM: Bear and Company,
    1984.
Swimme, Brian, and Thomas Berry. *The Universe Story.* San Francisco:
    Harper/Collins, 1992.
Toolan, David. *At Home in the Cosmos.* Maryknoll, New York: Orbis Books,
    2001.
Tucker, Mary Evelyn, and John Grim, eds. *Worldviews and Ecology: Religion,
    Philosophy and the Environment.* Maryknoll, New York: Orbis Books,
    1994.
Tvedten, Benet Br., O.S.B. *The View From a Monastery.* New York: Riverhead
    Books, 1999.
U.S. Catholic Conference. *Renewing The Earth: An Invitation to Reflection on
    The Environment in Light of Catholic Social Teaching.* Washington, D.C.:
    U.S. Catholic Conference, 1991.
Wessels, Cletus. *The Holy Web: Church and the New Universe Story.* Maryknoll,
    New York: Orbis Books, 2000.

INDEX